I WAS A CAPTIVE IN KOREA

5

I WAS A CAPTIVE IN KOREA

PHILIP DEANE, pseud.

Gerassimos Svoronos-Gigantes

NEW YORK
W · W · NORTON & COMPANY · INC ·

COPYRIGHT, 1953, BY GERASSIMOS SVORONOS—GIGANTES

FIRST EDITION

PRINTED IN THE UNITED STATES OF AMERICA

TO MOLLY

Contents

My THANKS to Philip Obank, for his encouragement, advice, and help.

CHAPTER 1

The Hopeless Battle

So THIS is Korea, at last. The shadow of the plane slips swiftly across the nude, eroded hills. Between the hills a column of dust marks the path of a convoy of American youngsters going up to close some gap. Ah, there's the field down there. Runway looks like a quarry. Two DC-4's sprawl in neglected wreckage. A wonder they can get a plane down at all.

"Sorry," says the pilot, as we touch down between the craters. "We're going no further."

"Aren't we going to Taejon?"

"Runway out of order. Only L-5's can land there now."

"How do we get there?"

"There's always the railway. Or you can try hitch-hiking. Anyway, that's your worry."

We search out the Press Information Officer.

"There's a passenger train tomorrow," the lieutenant tells us. "We can put you up here tonight. You can try your luck at the station with freight trains, but you'll probably take twenty-four hours getting there. These Gooks"—no

9

American seems to call the Koreans, friends or foes, anything but Gooks—"these Gooks run their trains backward half the time. Or you can try hitch-hiking. But have a bite first, anyway. No mess kits? I guess the chow boys will fix you up."

There are long lines of G.I.'s before the cook shack, and three immense sergeants are dishing out tinned food that has been warmed up.

"Want any more? Got enough smokes? Like any candy? Have some gum. Here, take a slug of this. No, never mind, we'll wash those things for you."

Generous, friendly, open faces, all smiling, all pink beneath crew haircuts. Kind, hospitable boys from Kansas and Kentucky, from Minnesota and Massachusetts, boys who find it natural to make a stranger feel at home. "The kind of kids you send to the movies when you want some quiet in the house," someone says. Back home, no doubt, it will be Mom going off to the movies now, to get away from the quiet. And these boys? They can't be tomorrow's corpses.

I am still confident and impatient—not quite so much so as I was yesterday when I arrived in Tokyo. I heard disturbing stories there, but I have flown 11,000 miles from Athens to cover this little war and I am anxious to get to it in time.

"Captain, I'm told you run the artillery reconnaissance planes. I'm a correspondent, from the *Observer* in London.

10

I've got to make Taejon. Have you anything going that way?"

"I've got two L-5's going out spotting. One's going to-ward Taejon. It could drop you there and refuel after the spotting. You'll have to stay in the air about three hours."

I tell him it would take me twenty-four hours by train.

"Okay, okay. I'll fill out a voucher for you. That's the plane, over there. Take this paper to the pilot. It'll be a good chance to take some mail over to Taejon. By the way, we've lost some L-5's lately. The Yaks like shooting at L-5's. Easier than trying it on the jets."

The plane is ticking over already. I hoist myself into the cockpit, hook on the parachute, and fasten the safety belt. It is a Piper Cub, an unarmed, single-engined observation plane, and the job of the pilot, Lieutenant John B. Stanton, from Exeter, Missouri, is to direct strafe attacks by Ameri-can fighters against enemy columns moving between American and South Korean positions along an axis run-ning from Chochiwon to Yongdong, moving towards the double-track railway which American troops have been defending in a bitter engagement. How bitter I do not yet know. But I know that the Communist thrust towards Yongdong is accompanied by an enveloping movement southwest of Taejon. The enemy is seeking to cut off the Americans in the Taejon salient and at the same time to gain control of the vital double-track railway from Taejon to Taegu.

An hour after we leave base we strike gold. That, at

11

least, is how Stanton puts it. Directly below us a large enemy column, complete with trucks, troops, and some strange, large objects optimistically camouflaged to pass for haystacks, is moving quickly down the middle of the road.

Stanton addresses some sharp, strange jargon over the radio to the code name "Utah Dogs." These turn out to be jet fighters, silver streaks that promptly whoosh out of the sky behind us. They are so fast, these jets, that they cannot always see their targets: they have to be directed. Non-chalantly piloting his fragile L-5 with one hand, Lieutenant Stanton directs the jets to their prey, and tells them: "Give 'em hell."

Hell is given, without stint. The silver birds swoop down to the road, and tiny orange flames blossom on the targets, to be followed by telltale mushrooms of black smoke. Again and again, the lieutenant from Missouri patiently, meticulously leads his performing Utah Dogs through their paces: his laconic words drop clearly into the pilots' ears, telling them when to bank, when to turn, and guiding them up to the very moment when the trigger has to be pressed. One after the other, eight trucks go up in the air, and the twenty or so others burst into flames. Then we have a last run on the "haystacks," parked now at the roadside. Smoke pours from them, disappointingly white at first, as if they really were haystacks after all. But when rockets are used on them black clouds billow into the sky.

Then we fly on to Taejon. The airfield there looks more like the vacant lot next door, where the neighborhood children play Gangs or Pirates, than an advance base of the mighty United States Air Force. To dodge the wrecks dotted here and there, Lieutenant Stanton puts down his Piper Cub with the selective delicacy of an alighting butterfly, and taxies over to the signal tower, avoiding the craters as casually as a London taxi-driver threading his way around Piccadilly Circus. A tall, lanky major with a .45 slung in an armpit holster stalks out of the unpainted building.

"Hiya, fellows." Texan vowels, Texan consonants, and a grip of iron. He seems glad to see us.

"When are you going to get this golf course cleaned up?" asks the lieutenant fresh from directing the destruction of an enemy convoy.

"When is Taegu going to send me some dozers and graders?"

"When they get some themselves."

"Same old story?" says the major.

"Same old story," says the lieutenant.

Then a burst of anger. "It's a goddam shame. Not a tank yet, not a three-inch bazooka, no mines. Sending those kids up the line like that's as good as sentencing them to death!"

The two officers walk along in front of me. They are talking quietly and I try not to listen, but fragments of sentences reach me.

13

"Companies . . . piecemeal . . . to stop whole divisions . . . Not enough artillery . . . one of our men for a hundred of theirs . . . The old man's holding on, but Christ knows how."

I get a ride in an ambulance that is taking four wounded men to Taejon. There is no room in the cab, so I squat between the stretchers. An American medic, a child looking scarcely sixteen, a child pale and shocked, is tending the patients. The two boys on the lower berths have abdominal wounds. They have the ashen complexion which accompanies an internal hemorrhage. "Water!" "Water!" "Water!" But you don't give water to someone with a hole in his belly.

The legs of the man in the starboard top bunk end at the knees. The medic is busy releasing the tourniquets periodically, letting some blood out, then twisting the cord again. The wounded man on the other top bunk has a hole the size of a fist through his right lung. It could have been a shell splinter, or a dum-dum bullet. The hole has been plugged with gauze.

The ambulance tears along, bumping fit to break the chassis. Speed is vital. If they can get to the hospital quickly enough . . . ? But it is also essential not to bump the wounded more than can be helped. Which is to come first? Try to drive fast, try not to bump. The driver serves both masters as well as he can.

One bump makes the medic lose his grip on the tourniquet he is manipulating. The femoral arteries throb and spurt precious blood. I stand up and try to lend a hand.

"I'll give him some more plasma. Here, hold this," says the young medic.

We are interrupted by the sound of drops, fat drops, splashing down rapidly one upon the other. Blood is seeping through an upper-bunk stretcher, plopping onto the naked chest of the man with the abdominal wound. Bumps open up wounds.

The young medic is weeping now. He is just trying to undo the bandage when the ambulance stops. Someone throws open the door. We are in a large courtyard, full of vehicles, of soldiers with bandaged arms and heads—the wounded who can walk. There is a large public building, its filth deodorized by gallons of disinfectant. Stretchers on the floor, in rooms, in corridors, on landings. Medics, haggard and sleepless, pass from dying man to dying man, callous only because they have been numbed by too much caring for other men's agony. Doctors operate ceaselessly, their hands bare, blood spattered down their fatigues. No rubber gloves, no white smocks here. Stitch this, clip that, sponge, stitch, clip, saw—faster, faster, faster, there are more waiting.

Outside, I find the young medic from the ambulance sitting down against a wall, his face in his hands. Thick tears streak the blood caked brown on his fingers, and disturb the flies.

15

"Here, pal, drink this." Drowned childish gray eyes look up. A sniff, then a bloodstained hand reaches for the flask cap.

"I'll fill it again. Have another."

As he drinks, I hear the story. The young medic and his four wounded were members of a first-aid team. The one with the hole in the lung was the doctor. A shell had hit the small farmhouse where the aid station operated. Only the gray-eyed youngster had not been hit. All but him and his four wounded had been killed on the spot. And his four wounded are dying now, in the public building at the end of their journey.

Forget it, Deane. I wash my hands and go to the P.I.O.

Taejon, in this disastrous Korean July of 1950, is a fetid, rat-infested town. The smell of human excreta is inescapable. You walk on the stuff in the streets. It is caked on the buttocks of the starved, squat little girls who play listlessly on the roadway. It is smeared on the few fresh vegetables that are on sale. It is splashed on to you by the wheels of a passing vehicle. You see it thriftily carried off, a cherished commodity, to fertilize the fields and to be mixed with clay for the walls of Korean hovels. But the stink is nothing to the human tragedy that is being played out in every street of Taejon. The town's normal population of about 100,000 is being swollen daily by the unending stream of refugees pouring in from the north. Wild-eyed peasant women in white, grown old before their time by unremitting labor, stagger along with tremendous burdens perched precariously on their heads. Their flaccid breasts sway jerkily with each step. They are carrying on their heads all that could be salvaged from their abandoned homes. And strutting Koreans in uniform push them into the gutter: for here civilians are brutalized by their own soldiers. Families with squalling babies huddle at the roadside, boiling a handful of grain in a rusty tin over a fire of straw. Two men seize a dog, put it into a straw sack and beat it to death with rhythmical slowness. They are making sure that the meat will be tender.

This is the provisional capital of South Korea, and the headquarters of the United States Forces. President Syngman Rhee and the South Korean Government had fled here from Seoul, ninety miles to the north, when the capital was overrun by the Communist hordes in the first few days of the irresistible Red sweep across the 38th parallel, the artificial frontier selected to divide the American and Soviet spheres of Korea when Japan surrendered in 1945. But there is no hope in this provisional capital; Taejon's turn is coming soon, and everybody seems to know it. Here a gallant general and five thousand men are trying to stem the Red tide from the north: fifteen divisions, four hundred tanks, thousands of howitzers, armored cars, antitank rifles. It is a flood tide of Communist soldiers, well-led, Russian-equipped, confident and victorious, overwhelmingly superior in arms and numbers, that is faced by the gallant general and five thousand men from

17

a far-off land. Men? Many of the G.I.'s in Major General William F. Dean's 24th American Infantry Division are mere kids of seventeen and eighteen who went straight from school into the army and only a few weeks ago were still enjoying their first tentative experiments in manhood in the heady role of occupiers of Japan:

"Gee, back in Sasebo I had a car, only a Ford, but a honey. You should have seen my little Japanese girl. Gee, she was a honey. Lived with me in my little villa. It was a honey, my little Japanese villa. Say, got any more of that liquor? Gimme a slug, will ya?"

This is your kid brother, who ought to be still at school. But back in Sasebo he has a Ford, a woman, and a honey of a villa, though he's only seventeen. Do you give another slug of liquor to your kid brother who ought to be still at school? Give him the slug. He may not know, then, what is coming to him, in five minutes, when his unit moves up to guard a sector of the Kum River—a platoon to guard six thousand yards of front on behalf of the United Nations.

The Kum River is the last natural obstacle between the invaders and Taejon. Along it, two under-strength American regiments, the 34th and the 21st, have been holding a seventy-mile front now for three days, falling back only when the classic Communist tactics of infiltration leave them with no communication lines. I am given a lift to the front by Major Wade Heritage, divisional surgeon of the 24th Division, who wants to see for himself how his boys of the Medical Corps are coping with the heavy batch of casualties. Fragments from Communist shells are flying around as we drive along the road from Taejon to Kongju, twenty miles away along the Kum. But it is not the shrapnel that is worrying the major, that provokes his muttered "Bastards!"

The major is watching the refugees pouring past us along the road. There are old men and women, some carrying babies, but there are also thousands of strapping young Koreans marching along in their midst, heads held high, arms swinging. They are the only ones with smiles on their faces.

"We should shoot them all," the major says. "I'll bet there's at least a pistol in every pack. They're the ones who shoot our boys in the back at night. We let them through in front of our eyes, and tonight we'll hear that the Communists have infiltrated our lines again. It's sheer suicide!"

As the shellfire gets thicker we come upon an advance aid station under the charge of Lieutenant Parker Pratt, who looks as if he will collapse at any moment now.

"They blew our aid station from under us near Kongju, sir," he tells the divisional surgeon. "They fired three salvos into it, and the boys had just brought in six wounded from the firing line. Christ, those kids had acted so cheerful, feeling their troubles were over now they were in the hands of the medics."

"You've been up here too long," says the major, patting

him on the shoulder. "How would you like me to send someone to replace you?"

"Oh, I'll be all right," says Pratt, and he walks off to meet a stretcher party bringing in a boy with a broken back. Pratt and his assistants have hardly slept for a week now, but not one of them wants to be sent out for a rest. That, they explain, would be "taking a powder on those poor bastards out in the line."

We drive on. For two miles, not a soul in sight. Then we are suddenly hailed from the ditch beside the road.

"Where do you jokers think you're going? Unless you're aiming to desert, I wouldn't move farther."

Lieutenant Macarver, a tough, sandy-haired Canadian with American citizenship, is sitting in the ditch, listening to his radio. He commands the Third Platoon of K Company, 34th Infantry Regiment, and is responsible for a front three miles wide—with only thirty-six men under his orders. We join him in his ditch and share the tin of fruit salad he is eating—in between dodging the shrapnel.

"I would go back now," says Macarver shortly. "We're the rear-guard platoon of the rear-guard company of the rear-guard regiment in this here shooting war, and any minute now we might have to greet some Gooks."

The divisional surgeon has to continue his rounds of the aid stations anyway, and I decide to stay behind with Macarver. As the major drives off, a report comes over the radio that two squads of North Koreans have infiltrated into the area. The Third Platoon is ordered to find them and bring back at least two for "the old man." Macarver details two squads for the job, and, since he is "so goddam short of men," agrees to my accompanying the patrol. I follow Sergeant Richard Coulter, from Morgantown, West Virginia, into the valley. In single, diagonal file, we comb the area, walking knee-deep in paddy fields, human manure sloshing into our shoes. We are completely without cover, for we are patrolling the bottom of the valley, and the Communists hold the hills. Some bullets ping overhead, but Korean guerrillas are notoriously bad shots, and no one is hit. Overhead, Mustangs and jets are flying continuously, and a small reconnaissance plane circles the enemy positions, occasionally drawing anti-aircraft fire and directing the fighters on to their targets. On the hills to the left and right of us we can see white forms hopping from bush to bush. We know they are watching us, probably radioing our movements, but not one of our weapons can reach them, and we walk on.

Gerald Nelson, a freckle-faced youngster from Halma, Minnesota, says to me: "Say, couldn't you find an easier way of turning a buck, or do you enjoy this kind of smell?" Gerald hasn't yet reached the age where a man has to shave, but he has the appetite of a man and a half, and eats half the lieutenant's rations, though that still leaves him hungry. He complains to me that the card he sent his mother for Mother's Day took weeks to arrive. Wayne Parsons, from Jenkins in Kentucky, keeps asking permis-

21

sion to kill a couple of suckling pigs for a barbecue after the action. Another Kentucky G.I., Charles Lee from Maysville, carries the platoon radio, and acts under fire as if he were back home fiddling with his homemade transmitter. These and others like them, who do not have mistresses to talk about, who try not to blush when the tough sergeants use bad language, these are the veterans now. They know what it takes. They will fight for these reeking paddy fields as grimly as if they were defending American home towns, where not long ago they were sitting at school desks and dating the girls. Their sergeant, who fought at Guadalcanal and in the Philippines, leads them now through the paddy fields, searching for "Gooks." I follow, trying to look unconcerned as we pass through dead villages, kicking doors open, flattening ourselves against walls, unable to do the job properly because the G.I.'s have been told to respect property, even at the risk of their lives.

Then we see the two squads of infiltrees—running up a hillside and scrambling into the bushes. They fire at us and we fire back, but the company commander has said that on no account must we leave the valley, as this will enable more Communists to infiltrate and cut the road.

Sergeant Coulter cannot resist the temptation. He sends some of us up the hill. Bullets fly, but they are off the mark, and we catch up with one of the Koreans, crouching behind a bush. He tries to make a run for it under the cover of his comrades' bullets, but Sergeant Coulter brings two of the Communists down at three hundred yards' range and the others stop firing.

When we get to our prisoner, he is unarmed and tries to give the impression, by sign language, that he is not a guerrilla. But a few feet away, under a bush, we find his gun—a Japanese-type Luger. With it is a clip of ammunition for a Japanese rifle, which we are unable to locate. Then the radio recalls us. When we get back, the lieutenant says, "Well, the old man wanted two Gook prisoners so they could keep each other company. I guess this guy will just have to be lonesome."

Late that same evening I am again with the Third Platoon of K Company, 34th Regiment, in the Kongju sector, when sniping starts from the hills surrounding our position. We answer the fire. The sergeant from West Virginia fires far fewer shots than any of the others: he fires only when he can see the telltale flash of a guerrilla rifle. A jeepload of ammunition passes, on its way to supply M Company, which is on our left, supporting the 63rd Artillery Battalion. A unit has pulled out of the fighting without permission, and North Koreans, in G.I. uniforms, have crossed the Kum River in strength at Mong Myon. The 63rd has been cut off, and its men have retreated, blowing up the breeches of their guns with grenades. Two companies, trapped, have taken to the hills to get out of Communist clutches.

We go by jeep to M Company's position, where everybody is tiptoeing around in the dark. Nobody will answer my questions: I am told to keep quiet unless I want to get killed. The ammunition jeep is being unloaded and reloaded by silent men, working quickly but noiselessly. Two wounded who cannot walk are loaded into the jeep too, and it tears off down the road through bursts of mortar shells. The road is untenable, so we make for a hill and disperse, moving along carefully. The Communists, who know we are heading south, keep firing mortar shells with proximity fuses. I feel a searing pain in my left shoulder, and my hand comes away wet when I put it there. It does not hurt at first, but soon the wound warms up, and I give myself an injection of morphine from the small pack I received before leaving for the front. The morphine dulls the pain and all other sensations: what happens during the remainder of the night I can remember, later, only hazily. (I remember trying to bandage up the wound as I ran along quickly for fear of being left behind. I remember hearing some of the men call out: "Sergeant, sergeant, which way?" and then further shouts as guerrillas and North Korean troops fired in the direction of the voices.)

After running back all night with M Company, I reach the road and meet up again with the Third Platoon of K Company. The boys are looking glum, but they raise a welcoming smile. I join them on an ammunition truck that is just behind a tank bringing up the rear of a retreating convoy. Every bridge is blown up by the engineers as soon as we have got across. Nobody talks much. Nobody even bothers to answer the snipers' fire, although we are sitting

24

on a ton of high explosives. Some of the men fall asleep in fantastic positions, oblivious to bumps and bullets. One man's hand rests on a can of explosives, his feet on another man's head. The engineers are slap-happy from too much blowing up, and they use twice as much explosive as is needed for demolishing the bridges: they provide a series of spectacular pyrotechnic displays to the accompaniment of mad shouts of joy.

At intervals we come across American soldiers lying asleep in the road, their shoes flung aside to ease their bleeding feet. They have reached the point in human endurance where exhaustion brings first heedlessness, then oblivion. We load them all on the truck, making them stand, packing them tightly so that they cannot fall out, and still they sleep, waking occasionally only to mumble some incoherent phrase. By now we have men clinging to the fenders and lying across the hood. The springs bump alarmingly and the engine complains as the driver forces the overloaded truck through the night at fifty miles an hour.

At last we are through. We reach the point where there are trucks and jeeps to shuttle us back and forth, and where the medics—themselves in need of medical attention—are ready to administer to the needs of the beaten youngsters as they are brought in. We are taken to the regimental aid station. Those with serious wounds are patched up as best the doctors can manage, then loaded into ambulances, shot full of morphine so that they will not feel the agony of the bumpy road, and sent back to the base hospital for urgent operations. Suddenly I have to lean against the wall of the bug-ridden Korean house that serves as dispensary, and the next second I am dead to the world.

The remains of the 34th Infantry Regiment are lying on the grass around a Korean hamlet. There are not many of them left alive. Only one out of three seems to have got through—through the nightmare woods where each shadow may hide a Communist tommygun. This has not been the kind of action you should have to face in your first week of war. It is the kind of action designed for those troops that are called "seasoned," that have been brought closer to the animal state by continuous danger and hazard, and have learned to sense as a beast senses.

"I don't get this."

There is always one among them to formulate the questions that are passing through the minds of all.

"What don't you get?"

"This—all this. They told us it was a sort of police action. Some police action! Some cops! Some robbers! What is this police action?"

"Didn't your officers tell you?"

"Naw. We don't talk of such things with Bob."

'Who's Bob?"

"Bob. You know Bob. Our lieutenant."

26

"Well, didn't Bob tell you?"

"Naw. Not sure he knows himself. You tell me. What's Communism, anyway? Why are we here?"

Go on, tell the kid. Tell him. Tell him about democracy, about the creed of Marxism-Leninism, about the United Nations. Tell him why the free world has decided to take a stand on this particular case. Tell him of the heritage that history has brought to his country. Talk about the price of liberty, the price of leadership. Explain it all, so that he may die understanding.

But I, too, am dog-tired. I, too, have just come through the nightmare wood, and my brain is befogged with fatigue.

"Say, they won't send us back in again now? The regiment's chewed up. They'll let us rest? They will, won't they? The sarge said that in the big show they always let you rest. They'll let us rest now. Maybe they'll send us back to Sasebo?"

Tell him. Tell him you've seen the order. The order that will send them back into hell in three hours, when the trucks have brought up more weapons. Tell him to take his rest now, before it's too late. Tell him the meal that's being cooked is as much to boost his morale as to fill his stomach. Tell him that besides the meal he'll get a can of tomato juice. Nobody knows why the tomato juice has been sent.

"Say, don't they know back in Tokyo that we haven't

got a chance. Won't somebody tell MacArthur? There's hundreds of them for each of us. And they've got them big Russian tanks. Our shells just bounce off. It's murder."

Yes, it's murder. They know it, and when it comes they will face it without a whimper, however much they grumble beforehand and however full of fear they may be. All great enterprises have to be launched on sacrifices. But why has it always to be the young that are sacrificed? Why did Iphigenia have to die at Aulis? "Greater love hath no man than this, that a man lay down his life for his friends." Fine words, comforting words. But these lives that are going to be laid down, they haven't been lived yet, they've hardly begun. Can't they have a stay of execution?

"Say, now you've got the million-dollar wound in your shoulder, you'll be going back to Tokyo?"

"No."

"Where then?"

"I'm staying here."

"You mean you're going back in there?" Incredulity.

"Yes."

"You crazy?"

"No. Got a job. I get paid for it."

"You mean you're going back in there just for a few greenbacks?"

Yes, for a few greenbacks, if you like to put it that way. But at least I know what I'm going back "in there" for. This kid doesn't know why he's going back in there. Just now, he doesn't know he's going.

28

Back in the Taejon P.I.O., I type out my story, and send it with a Reuters man who is flying back to Tokyo. Then I sleep for twelve hours before going for a walk around the town, still at this hour the headquarters of the United States Forces in Korea. But out in the streets everybody believes it is the last hour: Headquarters, says the unfailing grapevine, is pulling out. Usually impassive Koreans stand at the street corners in groups, stricken and stunned, whispering among themselves and watching furtively the movements of the Americans. From early morning the railway station has been blocked with refugees. This time they are on the way out. Trains pull out with swarms of human bees hanging from the steps, clinging to the roofs, even sitting on the locomotives, in a temperature exceeding 100 degrees.

By a bridge near a filthy makeshift hospital, a Korean soldier with a wooden gun stands guard—and pleads with every passing Yankee vehicle to take him away. The rich and the Government officials have gone already, bribing or bullying their way onto the departing trains. Now the poor are preparing to follow them, mostly on foot. The Koreans lock up their houses at night to keep out the evil spirits. Tonight, as I prowl around, doors are wide open, permitting glimpses of the inhabitants crawling around the floor, making up their pitiable bundles for the trek to the south. Staying behind are those who will welcome the arrival of the Communists and those, the majority, who feel they have nothing to lose.

News from the front is confused, and officers are unwilling to give information. The grapevine is sure that evacuation date is approaching, and the grapevine is right. Yet withdrawal does not come before the G.I.'s, severely outnumbered, have pushed back again and again the tanks, heavy artillery, and waves of expendable infantry hurled at the thin American line; it does not come before the bulk of the Americans have escaped encirclement, straightened out their line, retreated in orderly fashion under terrific fire; it does not come before the Americans have paid a heavy price for the time they have gained.

I hitch-hike to Taegu, and from there take the train back to the front at Yongdong, southwest of Taejon. As I sit crouched in a cattle car, worrying over what the staff officers in Taegu have told me, I figure that it is only twelve days since I was in the bar of the Press Club in Tokyo, listening to a star correspondent who had decided that Korea was no picnic. And, for the first time since I set foot in Korea, I begin to think about the world I have left behind, about the impressions of my journey out —I cannot believe that it was so recent. I think about my little flat in Athens and the familiar taverns where my wife and I meet our friends. I recall a farewell evening meal in Phaleron under an orange tree, the table with the checkered cloth, the sea lapping up almost to the legs of the table, and above, myriads of slivery-blue stars, like signaling friends, cool and aloof in the warm black velvet of the Aegean sky.

My memories run on. Constantinople: the Golden Horn, the Bosporus, the old walls, the minarets, little medieval precipitous streets, barred windows, the mystery of the veiled houris that persists though the veils have gone. Damascus, Basra, Karachi, Delhi, Calcutta, and Bangkok. Then beautiful, breathtaking Hong Kong, where three million Chinese live under the puritanical rule of the British, where there are licensing hours, where there is order everywhere and everything works well, where the large fortune holders of China make their last Asiatic stand, building astronomically expensive, vulgar houses on the rock of the peak, building factories and skyscrapers, and trading, trading madly, with the Communists who have brought them to bay here in Hong Kong.

And Tokyo, a sea of shanties broken by islands of lofty buildings. The shanties for the Japanese, the hardworking, clever, enterprising, canny, admirable, resilient Japanese; the lofty buildings for the Americans who brought them to their knees. Shattered dreams of empire and broken hearts. Live well, conquerors, with your stores, your cars, your privileges. Watch the vanquished bow to your Shogun each day at three o'clock. You are not unkind, you are not exactly hated, but you are watched constantly by millions of black, slanting eyes.

A pity they do not have a chance to see you as I have

seen you, here in this sorry land of Korea, where they themselves were conquerors and overlords for so long. A pity they cannot see how you behave when the tables are reversed, when you are up against greater odds than they have ever known themselves. They might understand you then, for they would see you not in the guise of an all-powerful Army of Occupation, to be tricked and kow-towed to, but as individual Americans who are up against it. Individuals like Colonel Stevens of the 21st Infantry Regiment, whom I heard lecturing his junior officers on how to get into a foxhole without losing dignity. "When you hear shells," he was saying, "you walk nonchalantly off the command post, walk to the foxhole or nearest ditch, and get down into it feet first without disarranging your uniform." Before he had time to finish, shells were already coming over. We all dived headfirst into the near-est ditch, except the colonel. From the ditch we watched him walk across to us, look down at us, and shake his head sadly.

Individuals like Major Heritage, the divisional surgeon, who went straight into surrounded Taejon to bring out his wounded because he felt he could not ask anyone else to do the job. Or like the Negro sergeant, a medic, who went into the firing line to pick up two wounded boys, and brought them safely back though he had lost his left arm in the process—and then went out again, and was shot dead. Or like the six boys who, within sight of burning Taejon, took out a locomotive and its terrified native crew

32

to prevent twenty carloads of ammunition from falling into enemy hands, and fought their way back with it through an enemy ambush, careering crazily down the track and shooting madly at the enemy on either side.

Or like my gallant general, Major General William Dean, of the 24th Infantry Division, whom I saw, immaculate in battle dress, directing bazooka fire in Taejon against tanks not fifty yards away. I do not know that on this very day, as I travel to Yongdong, Major General Dean is being officially listed in Tokyo as missing, having last been seen, as I had seen him, in action with his men against North Korean tanks. I shall not know for nearly three years what has happened to my gallant general, for at the end of my journey lies Yongdong, and Yongdong, for me, is the beginning of another story.

CHAPTER 2

Capture

I ARRIVED in Yongdong on the morning of July 23, 1950.
Shells from North Korean howitzers were crashing into
the town, disintegrating building after building. The advance headquarters of the United States 1st Cavalry Division was pulling out. Signal trucks and weapon carriers
were roaring south, dodging the craters and occasionally
disappearing for good in the flash of an explosion. Seven
miles to the northwest, on the main road to Taejon, the
71st Tank Company, under Lieutenant Bob Freeman, was
covering the retreat, and this was the only force available
to stem the tide of fifteen Red divisions pouring south.

Communist armor was reported moving to attack Lieutenant Freeman's force. I left headquarters by jeep to
cover the engagement, and three miles out of town we
came under sniper fire. We drove on. A few moments later
our crankcase was pierced, and the engine froze. We
dived for the side of the road, followed by bullets. A blond
G.I.—he could not have been more than eighteen—was
hit in the back. He screamed, "Mama!" I crawled towards

34

him. Blood was throbbing in torrents from his lips. I looked for his identity discs. He had none.

Fifty yards away three jeeps stood before a small farmhouse. We crawled the fifty yards through a shallow ditch, still followed by bullets. In the sunken kitchen of the farmhouse there were five G.I.'s. They were not firing. Two others were dead: their bodies were being used as sandbags. Ray Rothermel and Slim Devorak, both eighteen, who had ditch-crawled with me, took charge.

"Draw a bead on those snipers and let them have it."

Shooting over the threshold and through holes punched in the flimsy mud walls, the G.I.'s covered the enemy fire. One died, then another, then a third. The last of these, a tall, lanky child from the Middle West, was hit in the head. Lying on the blood-soaked earthen floor, my face not ten inches from his, I watched him die. The dying lasted ninety minutes. "What's it all about?" he had asked me before he was hit.

Bullets, like angry humming wasps, skimmed over us. Sometimes one would hit the inside of the cast-iron rice pot and whizz around eerily, like a roulette ball. The survivors' ammunition ran out.

"Never mind," said Devorak. "Bob Freeman will take us out when he withdraws. Hear his seventy-fives booming?"

A moment later the seventy-fives of Lieutenant Freeman's tanks were silenced. Then both Ray Rothermel and Slim Devorak were wounded.

"Deane," said Slim, shot in the hip, "see my folks and tell them I was not afraid to die."

"Shut up!" said Ray, a bullet in his abdomen. "We're not going to die. Deane's lucky. He'll get us out now."

I crawled out of the kitchen to one of the jeeps on the road. I tried the starter. The engine was dead. The next one was all right. As I jumped into the seat, bullets hit the windshield; it looked like a sheet of old mica in a kitchen stove. The car was facing the wrong way. If only I could turn it, get the kids in, and drive like hell for Yongdong, we might make it, as we had done before when we ran the Taejon gantlet. First gear, then reverse. Eternities passed. A bullet hit my right hand, and I looked unbelievingly at the blood spurting out. One never believes this sort of thing can happen—"not to me." First gear, reverse, first again. Four tommygun bullets hit my left thigh. I could still work the clutch. At last I called into the farmhouse, telling the two who were not wounded to bring out Slim and Ray. Bullets whammed into the engine and it died away. The tires collapsed. I crawled back into the farmhouse.

We lay there, our faces pressed to the blood on the floor, wincing helplessly as bullets missed by inches. We lay there numb and frightened, physically sick with our fright. Between the salvos, weird, guttural shouts came from all directions. The shouts came nearer. It was three o'clock in the afternoon when two Korean tommygunners jumped into our refuge and ordered us to our feet. Slim and Ray couldn't do it. Blinking absurdly at each report, the two little enemy soldiers fired bursts into the wounded boys. Between the survivors and freedom there was now an impenetrable curtain, the steel of our captors' tommy-guns.

We were marched out to the road, the three of us. First our watches were taken. Then our socks and shoes. We were stripped to our underpants (the Koreans seemed to like T-shirts). We were told to kneel and our hands were tied behind our backs with telephone wire. Six days earlier, after a local counterattack, some G.I.'s, stripped like us, their hands tied behind with telephone wire, had been found shot in the back of the neck, and all three of us knew it.

"It's awful to die so young," said one of the G.I.'s. "I'm not nineteen yet. There's so much to do. So much I should have done and didn't. So many people I've hurt, people I love, and now I cannot beg forgiveness."

They did not shoot us. Instead, they beat us, kicked us on the ground, and shouted at us—insults perhaps, but we could not understand. When that was over we were marched to a command post on the top of a leafy hill. There were other prisoners there—six of them. Two were severely wounded. At dusk we were ordered to stand up. The two who were badly wounded were finished off, this time with a pistol. Their executioner did not aim well. It took too many bullets.

In single file, almost naked, our hands tied behind, we

set off along goat paths, bare feet over loose stones. We marched. I stumbled. An American sergeant—his name was Frank, and I remember the wine-colored birthmark on his cheek—was walking behind me. Pushing with his shoulder, he kept me from falling over the precipitous edge, time after time. He was glad this was happening to him. The day he was captured he had received a letter from his wife telling him that she was getting a divorce, that she had sold the house and the car he had bought out of his savings as a soldier in World War II. Frank loved his wife, and he wanted to die. He died, but nobody could have wanted that way of dying.

Because of my wounds I was raging with fever, and the loss of blood accentuated my thirst. At dawn we stopped —for the first time—beside a muddy pool, and the guard indicated that we could have a drink. Flat on our bellies, we drank and drank. A lazy water snake, disturbed, slithered out into the grass. Then the march went on, through the day. Flies succeeded the mosquitoes of the night. The sun rose in a clear blue sky, drilling into our uncovered heads. And out of the sun, screaming, United Nations jet planes dived straight at us, spewing bullets.

Lying half submerged in a flooded rice paddy, we were shaken by terror out of the daze of exhaustion and sunstroke. You feel so much more helpless when your hands are tied behind your back, when you are bleeding, when in every village on the route you have been beaten and kicked in the scrotum by inhabitants to whom you have been offered as a sitting prey by your Korean guards. The silver birds passed, but we stayed in the paddy. When the beat of our pulses no longer filled our consciousness, we felt the thirst again. Rice paddies are fertilized with human excreta, but we drank, drank deep and dipped our burning heads in the stinking water. A shaggy, dusty buzzard dropped not six feet away from me and resumed the meal the pilots of the United Nations had interrupted. Under his claws were the remains of an American sergeant. We marched on.

Our heads down, we were fascinated by grotesque lumps of oozing flesh that kept placing themselves rhythmically before each other under our eyes. It was a shock to realize that they were feet. Our feet. And then the planes came again, and we lay again in the excremental bilge, and we drank it. Once our hands were untied and we were given a basket of food. The food looked black. As we put in our hands the flies rose, and the food was white. It was boiled rice that had fermented. We could not keep it down.

The boy walking ahead of me, who looked like a cross between Walt Disney's Bambi and El Greco's Saint Sebastian, and whom we called Florida, was thinking aloud:

"It's unfair. God-damned unfair. They sent platoons against whole divisions."

The march that had begun on Sunday the 23rd ended on Friday the 28th in a small valley near Suwon. Here was the Communist Army headquarters. An interpreter became excited when I told him I was a journalist. They marched me off to a small clearing and made me kneel. Standing before me was a man in jack-boots, breeches, and T-shirt. He had three "English-speakers" with him. As soon as I answered the question of one interpreter, the second said I was a liar, while the first translated to the interrogator. Then, immediately, the third interpreter asked another question.

First Interpreter—What plans have the Americans got?

A.—You don't think they'd tell them to a journalist?

Second Interpreter—You're a liar!

Third Interpreter—When are the Americans going to counterattack?

A.—I don't know.

First Interpreter—You're a liar!

Second Interpreter—Describe to us the rocket the Americans have which "homes" on the aerials of our tanks.

A.—I've never heard of such a rocket.

Third Interpreter—You're a liar!

There were about a dozen questions, each more unanswerable than the previous one. It wasn't that one could not be broken down by this fast-flowing third degree, but that one simply did not know the answers. Yet the interrogator persevered, putting the same questions in different words, in a different order, faster and faster, through his three interpreters, interposing threats that he would use the pistol in his hand. One became obsessed with keeping track of one's previous answers.

I fell asleep and, from my kneeling position, dropped onto my face. I awoke with a sharp pain in my left side. I had to kneel again. This went on from sunset until the black sky had turned to blue again in the east. The cocks were crowing. I remember wondering, absurdly, if the cock-a-doodles were their answers to some interrogating fox.

At last it was over. In a small hut near the clearing where the interrogation had taken place, I met a Lieutenant Thompson. He was a Corsair pilot from the U.S.S. *Valley Forge*, 27,000-ton aircraft carrier. While diving low to destroy a bridge with rockets, his engine had been hit by fragments from one of his own missiles. The oil ran out. The propeller stopped turning. Somehow, he managed to land in the nearby rice paddies. His radio was still working and he heard the pilots of the other two planes in his flight telling him to hold on. They were going to bring the helicopter around. Thompson checked his .45, got out of the cockpit, and waited, lying flat beside his now useless plane. Soon he saw six North Korean soldiers walking towards him, their tommyguns at the ready. Thompson took careful aim, and fired when the enemy was fifty yards away. One North Korean screamed, dropping his tommygun. The other five opened fire on Thompson. He answered the fire until he ran out of ammunition, but he did not score any more hits. He told me he felt nervous.

Then the Communist tommygunners advanced to the

41

plane. Thompson stood up, his hands above his head. Gesturing eloquently, one of the Koreans made Thompson understand that they were very angry with him for having fired at them. The speaker became worked up and his gestures turned to blows. The other four joined in. When I saw Thompson, he had a black eye and cut lips, and he told me the rest of his body was covered with bruises.

At Communist Army headquarters he had been interrogated ceaselessly for forty-eight hours. His interrogators kept telling him that he was a war criminal who had killed unarmed civilians, that he was guilty of crimes against humanity, and that he would be tried by a People's Tribunal and shot "any time now." He said that during the interrogation no physical violence had been used against him, and that the interpreters had assured him that the soldiers who hurt him would be severely punished.

"They told me they would try me today. I have never bombed or strafed any civilians. This was my first sortie, my first flight over Korea. They say they will shoot me. They keep calling me a liar. I'm so tired I can't remember anything. If you get out, tell my mother, will you? Tell her I love her very much."

Then they came and took him off for another interrogation.

I was put into a jeep and driven to Seoul. There, in a small Japanese villa, a flat-faced Korean in a Malenkov suit—buttons all the way up—tried to persuade me to broadcast over the North Korean radio, condemning the Americans. To make a broadcast, he said, was the only way I could let my wife know I was alive. He preferred not to comprehend that I could broadcast such an assurance without accusing the Americans of atrocities. He persisted for a whole day, giving me the first taste of the "brain-washing" technique that was to be applied much more insistently later on. In the end he washed his hands of me. He handed me the bloodstained fatigues of a dead G.I. and a pair of rubber sandals.

"You are not co-operative," he said. "You will be taken to Pyongyang. They can deal with you there."

The ride to Pyongyang was in a truck filled with documents and handbooks captured in the United States Military Mission headquarters in Seoul. I sat at the back, squatting on the bottom between piles of books. In each town or large village, we stopped. The sub-lieutenant in charge of the vehicle shook hands ceremoniously with the headman, and the population was gathered. Then I was brought up to the fore. Speaking with jerky motions, almost screaming the monosyllabic sounds of this guttural tongue, first the sub-lieutenant, then the headman, made long speeches, during which they frequently pointed at me. Each culminating climax invited screams from the crowd, who shook their hands in gestures I later learned to recognize as menacing. They spat, and slapped and kicked me.

A young police officer wearing spectacles spoke to me

secretively in English, saying that he was sorry for what happened, that he was a Christian.

During the first night of the drive the truck was capsized into a ditch. The little tommygunner in smelly sneakers who sat guarding me on top of the piles of books had his left thigh broken by the weight of the cargo. Because I had been sitting on the boards, between stacks of publications, nothing landed on me. I was only shaken. It was a deserted spot. The nearest village was miles away. I put the guard's leg in a splint. After that, the sub-lieutenant was kinder.

At dawn, gangs of villagers, in rags, arrived with straw, ropes, and spades. The truck was put back on the road. The driver, working with a sledge hammer, and with remarkable skill, straightened one of the wheels, which had buckled. We reached Pyongyang at four A.M. on Sunday, July 30, 1950. The truck drove up before the Ministry of the Interior, and I entered another world. I was marched into a huge office with a conference table and an enormous desk, behind which sat a man in shirt sleeves. Over him hung a poster with photographs of the North Korean Government. His own picture was on the right of Kim Il Sung's.

This was Korea's Beria, the Minister of the Interior. He waved me to the chair. The interpreter beside him started translating the questions, which were spoken in a quiet, even voice, while the unblinking, slanted eyes never moved from my face.

44

"What is your name? What is your age? What is your nationality? What is your profession? What identification documents do you carry to prove your statements?"

"All my papers were taken from me at the front."

"What else was taken from you?" He wrote down a detailed list. "We are not savages," he said. "We are civilized people. All this will be returned to you in good time." (I am still waiting.)

Then, from a delicate Chinese jug, he poured out a cup of milk, and pushed it across the desk.

"Drink," he said. It was my first meal in a week. He produced a box of Havanas. He waited till I had smoked about an inch.

"Who do you think started this war?" he asked.

I replied that I thought the North Koreans had attacked across the 38th parallel on June 25.

"Were you there?"

"No."

"How do you know, then?"

"I have interrogated witnesses, trying to trap them into contradictions. I have examined evidence, and it all points to the conclusion that you attacked."

He was silent for a moment, then poured out another cup of milk for me.

"Drink," he said. Then: "This war did not start on June 25. It started a long time ago. For years now the South Koreans have been attacking us and we have been repulsing their attacks."

45

"But this isn't just repulsing; this is conquering."

"They started that. You remember the time when they crossed the Parallel on the east coast and held a large part of our territory for days, until we drove them out with hard fighting. That was conquering, too. They also sent assassins and poisoners. They want to assassinate me." And the interpreter translated this, looking and sounding shocked at the thought that anyone should consider assassinating His Excellency.

"So," resumed the Minister, "we decided to terminate these provocations. Ours is a democratic government motivated by the interests of the people. We want peace. That is why, when we were attacked on June 25, we counterattacked on June 26 and crossed the Parallel with the purpose of eliminating the cause of all the trouble. What do you think of this?"

"I think your interpreter speaks remarkably good English."

"You," he said, "are a member of a responsible profession. You have to think and reason, and then you have to understand life. You are not fooled by appearances because you have to delve deeply into things. You have read Marx, haven't you, and Engels, and Stalin? Well then, you must be able to realize what we Communists are trying to do. You have read Dickens? You claim, I suppose, that you are an honest man. How can you reconcile intellectual integrity with what you must have seen going on around

46

you in England—oppression, poverty, and lack of justice?"

"Dickens wrote one hundred years ago. Things have changed."

"I would expect such an answer from someone else, but not from a journalist. You can't make me believe you are fooled by appearances. Do you not revolt against the lack of justice in your country?"

"An English judge allowed Gerhart Eisler, a prominent Communist, to make good his escape from the United States, because there is no provision in English law punishing people for their political beliefs. Is that lack of justice?" All this was said quite amiably, and the conversation went on along these lines for some time. Then the tone changed.

"I see," said the Minister, "that I have made a mistake. You do not have the broad outlook of a journalist. Perhaps you are not a journalist at all. Perhaps you are a spy."

"Would a spy get himself arrested at the front? Would he not, rather, come in as some kind of peace delegate?"

"Perhaps to allay our suspicions he might try to come in the way you came."

"And how could I, as a prisoner, communicate information to the outside world?"

"On your way up from Seoul you spoke to someone in English. Perhaps he was your contact."

"But what information could I have?"

47

"You are not to ask questions, you are to answer them. You had better prove you are not a spy."

The voice which was speaking these words in an unknown tongue was very quiet and even.

"Do you know what we do to spies?"

They had shot down wounded prisoners; they had treated the others in a way that hardly bears remembering; what would they not do to spies? I was very frightened.

"If you can prove your identity, if you can help us find out who you are in any way, then everything will be all right. We are not savages, we are civilized people."

It was very important for a frightened man to prove that he was not a spy.

"How can I prove it?"

"You can make a broadcast. We do not want you to say anything you would not write for your paper. We want you to condemn the American atrocities, their unjustified intervention in a civil war, and the fact that all this is contrary to the United Nations Charter."

"But that is not reporting. That is expression of opinion. I can't do that. In any case, my contract forbids me to broadcast for anybody."

"I see that you are making excuses. Perhaps you do not want to write a broadcast because you are afraid we might detect that you cannot write, and therefore that you are not a journalist but a spy."

"Look, I'm tired, I'm simply exhausted. I can hardly un-

48

derstand what you are saying. Even if I made a broadcast now, nobody would believe me, nobody would recognize my voice. Please may I rest?"

"Yes," said the Minister, "you may. We will talk of this later. When you have rested and made your broadcast, we shall give you medical attention. We cannot spare doctors. The bombing has caused so many casualties that we do not have enough medical staff. But after you make your broadcast, we shall find a doctor, I am sure. Your leg is infected, is it not? It would be a pity to lose it."

An incredibly ugly and savage-looking guard collected me from the Minister's office. I was sure he was going to be most unpleasant. He helped me solicitously down the stairs, brought out a towel and soap, and washed me when he saw I could not do it alone with one hand. Then he showed me a trellis-top table, covered me with a blanket, and squatted beside me. My last thought before I went to sleep was that he looked like one of the Buchenwald inmates. The name Buchenwald seemed to fit him, somehow. In the morning he awakened me with a bowl of rice soup and looked on while I ate. Then he washed me again. There was an air raid and I had to take shelter in a trench. I fell asleep. Later that day I was driven in a jeep out of the town to a ramshackle group of huts. While I sat waiting in a room, a bronzed, blue-eyed, barefooted man strode in purposefully.

"I," he said, in a firm parade-ground voice, "am Lord, of the Salvation Army. It's good to see you."

I nearly laughed. This was so much like the "Doctor Livingston I presume" routine of Spencer Tracy.

"I am Philip Deane, of the *Observer*."

We shook hands solemnly.

A few moments later, in another part of the building, a kindly giant with a soft Irish brogue helped me to lie down on the floor. "Relax," said Monsignor Thomas Quinlan, "relax, my boy, you are now with friends." I was in the camp for civilian internees in North Korea.

It was thirty years since Thomas Quinlan had left his native County Tipperary. A farmer's son, he had gone to the seminary and chosen evangelization as his life work. A few days before he was due to leave for his first post in China, this massive rugger-playing young priest was assailed by doubt. He went to his confessor, a Jesuit.

"Father," said the young missionary to be, "I am afraid."

"What about?"

"Well, in the missions I shall have to live with other priests, in isolated spots, and I am sure they will dislike me."

"Now what got that idea into your head?"

"I am not a good conversationalist. I never tell stories. I cannot talk."

"Ah," asked the old Jesuit, "but can you listen?"

"I think so, Father."

"Then you will be popular, to be sure. Everybody likes a good audience, and listeners, Tom my boy, even in our calling, are rarer than talkers."

So Thomas Quinlan went to China, applied himself to learning Chinese, trying to adapt his brogue to the four tones of the Peking dialect, made friends and converts, and built. Wherever he went, buildings went up for the glorification of the faith which moved Thomas Quinlan. Wherever there was building to be done, he was sent, and with his soutane tucked in his belt, his blue eyes twinkling, addressing his Chinese workers in a voice that remained Irish even in Pekingese, Quinlan carried bricks, mixed cement, carved stones. Then, cleaned up, he strolled down the market street, exchanging elaborate greetings with the townspeople. Everybody knew him.

From China, he was moved to Korea, where finally he became prefect apostolic of the province whose capital was Chunchon, some miles south of the 38th parallel.

There, living in his tiny room in a Korean house, Monsignor Thomas Quinlan made the plans for what he knew he had to build before he could return to Ireland on leave —a cathedral, his first. It had to be a basilica, with beautiful woodwork, stained-glass windows and a golden roof. It had to be on top of the hill, so that all could see the cross.

Monsignor Quinlan visited the American military governor of the province (this was before the military administration withdrew). The next day bulldozers and graders were working on the site. With his Chinese contractor by his side, the Monsignor watched before leaving hurriedly to visit his sick.

The foundations were laid, the scaffolding went up, the

dressed granite blocks rose higher and higher, skirting the embrasures of the doors and windows.

Finally the time came to place the golden roof. Many of his flock of twelve thousand came to see the first shining sheets being laid. Why not watch? They had paid for them out of their minute incomes in response to the call of this man who was a big man in his Church and yet lived as simply as they.

Every morning, after saying his prayers and before going to say Mass, the Monsignor stood in the courtyard of his Korean hut and looked at that building on the top of the hill. He would dedicate it on August 15, 1950, in less than two months' time. The thought of the dedication service made him happy and made up for other thoughts —thoughts about things that were not going well in the town, about people who were being arrested for no reason, about bribes, graft, misery, unhappiness. They were sad thoughts, thoughts which made the Monsignor's eyes lose their twinkle until they were turned again to the top of the hill, to the golden roof.

There were only the windows to put in, and the pews. It was June 25, 1950. "Sure and everything will be fine by the feast of Our Lady, praise be to God."

Some minutes later, shells started falling into the town. One fell in the courtyard of the Monsignor's house. A shell splinter hit him on the jaw. Ignoring the blood—all this was told me by one of his priests—he rushed out to administer first aid to others. When that was over, tired, apprehensive about what might happen, uneasy about what he had guessed from the movements of the officials, he turned for comfort for the first time since the bombardment began towards the golden-roofed building on the hilltop.

In the shiny brass plates, in the dressed granite, there was a gaping wound. Without saying a word, his mouth set, striding fast against a freshening wind, the Monsignor went to inspect the damage, followed by his assistants.

They stood a little behind him while he ran his calloused hands over the blackened stone, the twisted brass, the smoking wood so lovingly chosen.

Then, turning, he walked down the hill.

"That gunner!" someone muttered angrily. "If I could get my hands on him . . ."

"Hush, hush!" said Monsignor Quinlan. "Remember, his mother loves him, the poor misguided lad."

South Korean loudspeaker vans were driving through Chunchon.

"Be calm. Do not worry. Our glorious army has repulsed the brigands of Kim Il Sung, thrown them back across the Parallel, and is pursuing them now with bayonets. Ten thousand cheers for our great President Syngman Rhee. Ten thousand cheers for our valorous army."

Twenty minutes later, the Communist troops entered the town.

For some days no one molested the Monsignor and Father Francis Canavan of County Galway. They went on saying Mass every morning, before a depleted congregation of the faithful, young and old. Once a Red Army officer went up to the Monsignor and asked him whether he was an American:

"If you are not an American we have no quarrel with you, and we have no quarrel with your religion."

The next day, as Monsignor Quinlan was celebrating Mass, some shots were fired through the door of the tiny church. The congregation fell to the ground. Two old women started wailing. Four members of the North Korean security forces walked in. With the butt of his rifle one of them smashed an image of the Virgin Mary. Another flung the chalice from the altar to the floor. The congregation and the priests, their hands held high, were marched out into the courtyard. There the Communist noncommissioned officer in charge screamed at the Koreans he had found in the church, especially the young ones, for listening to the lies of the "foreign devils."

Then, cocking his gun and turning to Father Canavan, he said: "I am going to shoot you. Keep your hands up and walk to that wall, then turn to face me and I will shoot you."

Father Canavan walked to the wall and turned. The n.c.o. aimed his gun at the young Irishman for a few moments.

"Are you afraid?" he asked.

Father Canavan did not answer.

"You are going to die," said the n.c.o. "Can your God

54

save you? Can he stop me from pressing the trigger of my gun?"

"If you press the trigger," said Father Canavan, "it is because my God, who is also yours, wants you to press the trigger."

The n.c.o. lowered his gun.

"You see," he said, "your God cannot make me press the trigger if I do not want to press it."

Later, imprisoned in a filthy cell, the Monsignor knelt to pray. The warden flung the door open and pushed the muzzle of his gun into the Monsignor's ribs.

"Stop that," he said, "you have been liberated by the People's Army. Don't be superstitious. Stop it or I'll shoot you."

"Sonny," replied Monsignor Quinlan, "I've been praying like this since I was seven, and I am not going to stop just because you say so."

Of course, there were interrogations. A major (whom we were later to know as "the Tiger") had taken over as governor of the Chunchon jail. In between discussions on theology, the major and his subordinates tried hard to get confessions out of the Monsignor and Father Canavan. The central theme of the confessions required by the Communists was an admission that the priests had seduced the young girls who attended the church. Unable to get confessions out of the Monsignor and Father Canavan, the Communists interrogated the Korean Christians, confronting them occasionally with the captive priests.

Not one member of the flock yielded to threats, intimi-
dation, and blows. No one gave hostile testimony.

A Communist—a carpenter, who had been incarcerated
and tortured by the South Koreans—burst into the prison
governor's office one day when the Monsignor was being
interrogated.

"This man," said the carpenter, pointing to Thomas
Quinlan, "is a good man. I who am a Communist tell you."

"Mind your own business," said the prison governor.

After staying some days in the Chunchon jail, Monsignor Quinlan and Father Canavan were taken to the Seoul
jail and then to the camp for foreign civilian internees in
North Korea. It was here that I met them. It had been a
school building, and had consecutive rooms connected by
a long corridor. There was the British room, the miscel-
laneous room, the French room, the women's room, and
the American room. The groups occupying these rooms
were not allowed to communicate with one another. We
were not allowed to talk loudly. We were not allowed to
go to the lavatory without permission from the guards. We
were all desperately hungry, because the food consisted of
three teacupfuls of rice a day and three teaspoonfuls of
turnip-top juice.

An incredibly dirty Korean brought us water in a bucket
that normally stood by the neighboring pigsty. We all, of
course, had dysentery, but there was no treatment. There
was a doctor in the American room, yet the guards would
not allow us to consult him. They would never accede to

anyone's requests—except Monsignor Quinlan's. His Irish charm worked even on North Korean prison wardens. As a special favor to him, they allowed Dr. Ernest Kisch, of Vienna, to look at my wounds, to squeeze out the bullets that were near the surface, to remove as much of the infection as he could, and to pack the wounds with some sulfanilamide powder which a French chargé d'affaires had somehow managed to bring with him into internment. That was a whole week after the North Koreans captured me.

Of all the tragedies of this internment Dr. Ernest Kisch's was, perhaps, the most ironical. Until the Anschluss in 1938 he had been a fashionable physician in Vienna. His was a brilliant clientele of people who liked his knowledge and his ready wit. And then he found himself forced to wear sewn on his clothes the yellow star that marked him as a Jew. He was sent to Dachau, and afterwards to Buchenwald. In 1939, some friends—diplomats—managed to get him released. The tired, almost broken man, was offered employment in the Shanghai Methodist Hospital from where he went to the American Methodist Hospital in Kaeson, right on the 38th parallel in Korea.

At 5 A.M. on the morning of June 25, 1950, North Korean tommygunners jumped into his room and dragged him, in his underwear, to the prison. There he found the other members of the American Methodist Mission. All day, as is the rule in Oriental jails, Dr. Kisch was made to squat. He was shouted at, starved, and taken to the lava-

57

tory only once a day. Then, packed in a cattle car with so many people that one could only sit with legs drawn up right under the chin, he was made to wait for days in Seoul station, forbidden to get out even when United Nations planes strafed the sidings. Miraculously he was not hit, and arrived finally in the dilapidated school where he treated me. Dr. Kisch's country, Austria, is not a member of the United Nations. Even in the time of her empire, she had never attacked Korea in any way. Dr. Kisch, who for a pittance had devoted his skill to the service of the Koreans, who had been imprisoned by the Nazis for being a Jew, was now imprisoned because he was not a Communist. During the captivity his greatest hardship, he said, was not being allowed to use his medical knowledge to help anyone. Dr. Kisch, who had survived Dachau and Buchenwald, died of starvation in North Korea.

The oldest of the civilian internees was eighty-two— Father Paul Villemot, who had come to Korea when he was in his early twenties, and had hidden from persecution, made converts, and eventually built cathedrals. He was bedridden when the invasion came, refusing to go home, wanting to die in his beloved Korea, to be buried like the old Korean men he so resembled now. He was literally dragged to the prison, fed on boiled barley once a day, packed into a cattle car, and finally dumped on the bare verminous floor of the school where we were interned.

In another room there was a breast-fed baby. His

mother's milk had stopped, and he could not digest the other food. As an immense concession the guards gave the mother some hot water. Inexplicably, the mother's milk came back. The baby lived.

At night, the mosquitoes, lice, and bugs kept us awake. It was a relief to be called away for the interrogations that went on constantly in another part of the building. These were carried out by minor officials who had forms to fill out. "What's your name? Christian names? Aliases? Father's name? Mother's name? Their ages? What countries have you ever visited? Write down exact dates of arrival at and departure from . . ." Then: "What other relatives have you got? Cousins, aunts, uncles? Do you expect us to believe you have no more?" (In Korea, because there are only about a dozen surnames and many of the given names sound alike, people are identified by the names of their relatives.)

It was the French who started the fashion of inventing relatives.

"The little men were so insistent," said M. Georges Perruche, who had been French chargé d'affaires in Seoul, "that I felt it would hurt their feelings if I stopped giving them names."

Somewhere in the archives of North Korea there is a voluminous dossier about M. Perruche's mythical schizophrenic aunt, who paints pictures while riding a bicycle and gets arrested for breaking the traffic regulations, whose brushwork was much influenced by "Lenin's treatise on art," and who renounced her realistic naturalism "pour l'acromégalisme sénile."

"Please," asked the interrogator, "could you tell me how to write this? What is it?"

"A French art school," said Perruche.

"You are decadent," said the large-eared, bespectacled young Asiatic, shaking his head pityingly.

Humor was a rare and precious commodity, and the few occasions on which it could be displayed remain stamped on my memory, with other small human details.

"Francis, Francis," said Monsignor Quinlan one night to a learner of bridge, "when I say two clubs after passing the first time, it is not a forcing bid."

Every night, an interrogator pressed me to broadcast. Five days after my arrival at the Pyongyang school, on August 4, 1950, a car came to fetch me.

"We are taking you into town," said the escorting interpreter, "because here you are afraid to broadcast. Your compatriots will not let you, especially Captain Vyvyan Holt" (the British Minister in Seoul, now an internee).

They took me to a Japanese house in the town, where I was seated at a large table facing three interrogators. A very large electric lamp hung down six inches from my face. There were blankets over the windows, and it was very hot. The man sitting in the middle started talking:

"You came to Korea with the American invaders. You were captured at the front. You were treated kindly—not like the Americans treat prisoners. You have seen the de-

struction. American planes bomb our hospitals. This is
civil war. They have used their automatic majority in the
United Nations to bring in their satellites against us. Britain is a satellite. We do not fight Britain. Our ships do not
bombard British shores. Our men have not invaded your
country. Why do you come here to fight us? Do you not
think war is unnecessary? Do you not think that a small
country like ours should be allowed at last, after fifty years
of slavery, to decide its own fate?

"Do you think the English people—the mothers and
wives especially—want young Englishmen killed? You are
married. Do you think your wife liked your going to Korea? And how do you think she feels now, without news
from you, not knowing whether you are alive, listening to hear from the radio that you are not dead? You
would like to hear from her also, would you not? We can
get a telegram from her in a few hours. We would like to
do that for you. Now if you will speak on the radio, if you
will condemn the atrocities which you have seen, if you
will speak of the dead women and children, then your wife
will hear your voice and she will be happy. And we will
bring you a telegram from her.

"No, you cannot just broadcast a message. This is wartime. We cannot waste an important propaganda weapon
like our radio for personal messages. You understand that,
don't you? I'll tell you what, if you broadcast as we tell
you, if you prove to us that you are what you claim to be—
an impartial reporter—if you co-operate with us in expos-

ing the Anglo-American crimes, then we will liberate you.
You are a civilian, we have no reason to keep you here. We
are not your enemies. We help those who help us. Do what
we ask, and we will send you through China to Hong
Kong. No, we cannot send you first, you must broadcast
first, we cannot trust you. How can you trust us? But we
are empowered to speak on behalf of the People's Government. I see you do not trust us. Yet you have no choice. Do
you think your wife would thank you for dying here? Do
you think it is worth while being pigheaded? Can you not
rid yourself of your prejudices for a while? Let your mind
be free. Give us the chance to explain.

"After all, you should look at both sides of the picture.
No, you did not have exact information about us before.
Your press is biased. You have heard Moscow broadcast
and read Communist books? And you were not convinced? Don't you see that your environment, those people you call your friends, all the things around you, were
bound to influence you against understanding us? Intellectual honesty, you know, is a difficult achievement. It is
so subjective. Why do you refuse to consider our point of
view? We are a small poor country. Some of our institu-
tions might shock the Western mind. I am a professor of
ethnology, I have studied in Berlin and London, and I
know how the West thinks.

"I am not a Communist myself. You do not approve of
our methods? But we have to adopt emergency measures.
We are centuries behind. We cannot, for the sake of the

suffering people, wait for the slow process of reform. Can you justify, from the standpoint of humanism, the starvation of a child? You say neither can you justify aggression? But we did not attack. We can prove it with documents captured in Seoul. We are preparing a book on the subject."

On and on. Then the change of tone.

"I am afraid that the Minister was right. You cannot be a journalist. If you were a journalist you would not mind reporting facts. We've heard this story about your contract. You are just dodging the issue. You are afraid to write because you cannot write, and you are afraid we will find out. Come to think of it, your accent is not completely English. On your way from Seoul to Pyongyang you talked to a man in police uniform. We cannot find him. We believe he was your contact. Our headquarters were bombed the next day. You must have given away the location. Who was that man? We have ways of making you talk, you know. We are not savages, we are civilized people. We are trying to be kind, but you realize that we must think of our country and its security. Who was that man? Of course you'd say you don't know. What will happen when we catch him and confront him with you?"

Yes, what would happen when they confronted me with the poor, kind wretch of a policeman who had made the mistake of whispering, "I'm sorry. I'm a Christian"?

"You," the ethnologist continued, "have a chance of saving your life, of making your wife happy, of becoming free

63

again. You refuse to take this chance. What happens to you from now on will be your own fault. We are not savages, we are civilized people. We do not want to ill-treat you, especially if you are a journalist. But we cannot find the man with whom you spoke. So you must prove that you are not a spy. If you don't, then on your head be it."

I felt sure, then, that they would use physical violence, and I told myself that I would give way at the first signs. But they did not touch me. They just went on—the three of them in relay—alternating threats with cajolery, abandoning the spy theme to appeal to my objectivity as a reporter, interlarding their talks with Marxist jargon, building up elaborately complicated arguments which sounded so logical except for some flaw. It was awfully important to keep finding that flaw, to keep control of the facts one had known and which were being washed away by the ceaseless talk.

CHAPTER 3

Interrogation

I HAD been brought to the house in Pyongyang late on the evening of August 4. At the edge of the blankets hanging before the windows, hours later, I saw the light of day come in. I saw the signs of dawn that way three times during the ceaseless interrogation. Then I remembered nothing more—until I came to, in a bed, with an English-speaking Korean police captain sitting by my bedside.

"You have been very ill," he said, "and I have orders that you should not die. The correspondent of the *Daily Worker* cabled London about your capture, and your newspaper is making much noise about you. They have also asked at the United Nations for your release. I think you must be important. And you must be well."

After my three-day interrogation and subsequent illness, I was kept in the North Korean capital, being fed milk, eggs, and Coca-Cola, to recover. I was practically unguarded. During air raids, the occupants of the house would scuttle off to the shelters without insisting that I should follow them.

I didn't follow, because I wanted to investigate the three

radio sets in the house, none of which appeared to work. By changing some of the tubes around, I got one of the sets functioning, and the raids becames an occasion for rejoicing. I would tune in to the B.B.C. Overseas Service, to the Australian Broadcasting Service, and to the American Forces Network. Thus I heard about the birth of Princess Anne to Queen Elizabeth (then Princess Elizabeth) and about the extra beer that was being given to the British forces in Korea to toast the occasion. That day, a prisoner drank her little Highness' health in looted Coca-Cola, for there was nothing else. I heard also that the United Nations forces had stabilized the tiny Pusan bridgehead that they were holding.

I heard of the tremendous preparations being made for the counterattack, of the death of two friends—Ian Morrison, of the *Times*, and Christopher Buckley, of the *Daily Telegraph*—and I listened to baseball results, hoping that I would get the chance to tell some American about them. Once, over the air, came "Take It from Here," with Joy Nichols, Professor Jimmy Edwards, and Dick Bentley. For the first time since my capture, hearing those three dear fools of British radio, I laughed and laughed. I want to thank them for that. Most broadcasts I could not hear completely, for as soon as the all-clear sounded I had to dismantle my repairs lest the Koreans discover my secret.

The house I was kept in appeared to be a distribution point for loot. A succession of trucks would arrive with personal effects that had belonged to the foreign colony in Seoul. Diminutive Korean police officers would try on American zoot suits (accidentally achieving an overcoat effect), surrealistic ties, and rimless spectacles which completely distorted their vision. Then the alert would sound, and in their outsize regalia they would solemnly and slowly leave the room. I watched them from the window. As soon as they thought they were out of my sight they would run for the shelter, only to reappear after the raid to assure me earnestly that they had stood outside watching the planes all the time.

From my window I could see the river and the two wooden bridges being built across it. The water of the stream was very green. The interpreter who was in charge of me claimed the color had not always been the same.

Once upon a time, he said, there was a very beautiful young Korean girl in Pyongyang, living by the river. In the neighboring house there was a young man who loved her very much; and she loved him. But he was poor, and the father of the girl would not allow them to marry—not until he was given a substantial gift. So the young man left Pyongyang to make his fortune. He went far away into the mountains, he braved the tigers and the wolves, and suffered from the cold of the winter. He dug the earth and took from it precious stones—emeralds.

With his priceless treasure in a bag he went back to Pyongyang, straight to the home of his beloved; but she was not there, and her father would not answer any questions; he would not—even though avaricious—consider a

67

gift of emeralds in exchange for information. Lovesick and desperate, the young man roamed the city trying to find his beloved. It was many months before he saw her standing on the top of a cliff by the river. They looked at each other with tears in their eyes. She told him that her father had sold her to a Japanese merchant, and she was so unhappy that she was going to kill herself. They both knew that it was hopeless. If they tried to run away together they would be hunted down and killed, for once a father had given his daughter away no one could do anything about it. And with one last fond look at her lover, the beautiful young girl threw herself off the cliffs into the rushing waters below. The young man knew then that he, too, could not live, and before killing himself as his beloved had done he threw into the river the now useless precious emeralds.

"And that is why," said my guardian, "the waters of the Tedong Gang are green."

"But fathers cannot do this sort of thing any more," he continued. "Now we have done away with the superstitions of the past and the bad old customs. Our Democratic People's Republic, under the guidance of our great leader and teacher Stalin, and in accordance with the orders of General Kim Il Sung, has emancipated women. If a father tries to make his daughter marry against her will, he goes to jail for a year. And we have divorce by mutual consent, the parents being jointly responsible for the maintenance of the children. The women are being educated. Every-

68

body is learning to read—young and old. Soon everybody
will be able to read the newspaper, the speeches of Kim Il
Sung, and the great works of Stalin, Lenin, Engels, and
Marx."

"Do you read those?"

"Oh yes, every day. Let me show you my notebook.
You see here I have copied Stalin's speech to the eight-
eenth congress of the Communist Party. He predicted
everything that would happen, because he based himself
on the scientific laws of social development discovered by
Marx and Engels."

"But on the basis of those laws, Marx and Engels did
not predict imperialism as a phase in social development,
and they said the socialist revolution could be successful
only if carried out simultaneously in the major industrial
countries. They also said that it would happen first not in
Russia but in the West. Doesn't that make you suspect
there might be something wrong with these laws?"

"Lenin raised the teachings of Marx and Engels to a
higher level."

"You mean he changed them, as Stalin has changed the
teachings of Lenin."

"No, no. The teachings were not changed. They were
explained to us who could not understand them by these
great men, who raised the teachings of their masters to a
higher level."

"Am I correct in assuming you think it is not possible to
understand Marx?"

"Not for simple people like us. One must have a great mind to understand such writing."

"You do not understand it, yet you admire it? Can you admire something you do not know?"

"Our leaders, who are great men, understand Marx and they tell us about him. He must be great if our leaders, who are taking us to victory, think he is great. And, in any case, his ideas must be big, because small men like me do not understand them."

"Tell me, have you always been a police officer, and where did you learn such good English?"

"I studied in Japan, then came back to be a schoolmaster."

"That is a fine profession. Are you going back to it after the war?"

"Oh no. Being in the people's security forces is much better."

"Why?"

"I think it is more important."

"More important than training the future generations?"

"Yes. We cannot train the future generations if we do not defend our Democratic People's Government against its enemies."

"But I thought your government had the support of the people, and had no enemies."

"You were wrong to think so. Have you not read what the great Stalin has said about the survivals of capitalism and how hard these fight against socialism? Well, here we have survivals of capitalism and of feudalism also. You see, the government carried out an agricultural reform, confiscating, without compensation, the property of the big landowners and giving it to the peasants."

"Is this land now the property of the peasants?"

"No, it belongs to the State, but the peasants can have it for their lifetime."

"And what happens to their children?"

"Adjustments are made every year in the distribution of the land. People with large families have more land, and when a male child reaches manhood he also is given land and can start farming on his own."

"And the peasants pay no rent to the government?"

"They pay no rent, only taxes. The average yield of an acre is assessed, and the peasants have to give up twenty-five per cent of their crop to the government. In exchange they receive fertilizer at very low prices and can buy agricultural implements at the co-operative store. The government must take this twenty-five per cent to provide for the police, the army, the civil servants, and the factory workers, who buy what they need in government stores."

"Can other people buy in the government stores? Can a merchant buy there, for instance?"

"No, they have to buy on the free market."

"But the peasants can buy in the co-operative stores?"

"Only fertilizer and agricultural implements."

"How do they buy other things: clothes, shoes, lamps, kitchen utensils, and the like?"

71

"Well, as the government takes only twenty-five per cent of what they produce they can sell what they don't need from the remaining seventy-five per cent on the free market, where the merchants and other peasants buy what they need."

"Are the prices controlled on the free market?"

"Of course not. It is free. The law of supply and demand applies."

"How do you reconcile that with Marx's theory of value based on the amount of average human labor?"

"That is for the socialist society. We have not reached socialism. We are in the stage of the Democratic People's Republic, as Comrade Mao Tse-tung describes it in the *New Democracy*. Have you read it? Well then, you know how the classes will be gradually eliminated. We still have the small industrialist class, the merchants, the peasants, and the proletariat. We will co-operate with the first two classes as long as they behave in the interest of the nation. They have been promised the protection of the law; but as soon as we advance to a new stage we shall eliminate those two classes, starting with the small industrialists."

"As the NEP men, the merchants, and the kulaks were eliminated in Russia?"

"Yes."

"Coming back to this economic system of yours, you say the merchants and peasants have to buy most of their consumer goods on the free market. Are not many of these consumer goods produced in State-owned factories?"

72

"Yes, they are—cloth for instance, shoes, cigarettes, drugs, electric-light bulbs, most of the soap, soybean oil, soybean sauce, and many other things."

"How do all these products get to the free market?"

"The government sells them to the merchants."

"At controlled prices?"

"I am not sure. There is a minimum, I think, but if the demand is great then the government raises the prices. It's a free market, so the rule of supply and demand operates."

"And how about Marx's definition of value?"

"Oh, that is only for socialism. We have not reached socialism yet."

"I thought Marx's definition of value was one of those fundamental laws of social development which apply in all forms of society."

"Oh no, I am sure Marx did not mean that."

"But you said you did not understand Marx."

"Our leaders understand him, and they would not act against the laws of social development which Marx discovered."

"They would raise these laws to a higher level?"

"Yes. They do so every day. Of course, it is very difficult now. You have destroyed all our factories. We had huge chemical and metal plants. We are fighting fifty-three nations. For the first time in history, a small country like ours is fighting against more than half the world and we are winning, without outside help. There are no Russian soldiers fighting in North Korea as there are Americans in

South Korea, and all the armaments we have we bought before the war, in 1948 in fact, from the Russians. Nobody helps us and we fight alone against the world."

"I saw some Russian officers driving past in their cars yesterday; what are they?"

"We have diplomatic relations with the Soviet Union. They have an embassy. What you saw was probably the military attaché and his staff."

"It must be a big staff."

"The Soviet Embassy is a big embassy."

"You mean they have a large number of advisers for you?"

"No. Our Kim Il Sung and all the top men in our government have been trained by the Russians. The chief of our department—you have met him—during the Japanese occupation was working for the Russians, collecting information and doing sabotage. He is a very clever man. He has studied in Germany. We admire him very much. He is only thirty-four and he is a colonel. He will go very high. He was trained by your priests, German Benedictines, but he soon understood the falseness of their teachings and studied Marx in Berlin."

"Now you mention the Benedictines, did you not put them in prison last year?"

"Yes, they were spies. We found wireless transmitters in their building. It was taken away from them and is now an agricultural college."

"And where are the Benedictines now?"

"They are in a correctional farm, reforming themselves with work. Work is the greatest necessity for man, Marx said in his critique of the Gotha program."

"You know, some people might consider this imprisonment of the Benedictine fathers as religious persecution."

"There is no religious persecution in our country. Everyone is free to have any religion he likes."

"But you do explain to the children that religion is superstitious, unscientific?"

"Of course. We have freedom of anti-religious propaganda. We have freedom in everything. Even in trade."

"This freedom of trade, does it include foreign trade?"

"No. That is a State monopoly. The State sells the imports in the co-operatives to the people who are entitled to buy there, and sells them also to the merchants on the free market."

"On the basis of supply and demand?"

"Of course. This selling to merchants is a good way of taxing them. You see, they are full of capitalist survivals. They would try to cheat the government. In this way we take their money before they earn it and we are sure to get it. It is better for the merchants even, this way, because we do not spend money on tax inspectors."

"You spend it on agitators and propagandists."

"Yes, they are very necessary to raise the standard of political consciousness of the people, especially our peasants, who are very backward."

"And how about raising the standard of living?"

"But we do. We only take twenty-five per cent of their crop."

"And, since the State holds the monopoly of so many products, including all imported goods, you overcharge them for everything."

"No, we do not. We have their interests at heart."

"I thought you said that the law of supply and demand applies. In a monopoly market, for prime-necessity goods, this means very high prices."

"You think like a capitalist. I will bring you a good book to read. Now I must go."

"Just one thing—I still think the peasants risk exploitation by the merchants."

"Well then, they can join collective farms, and be entitled to co-operative-store privileges."

"So you are going ahead with collectivization?"

"Oh no. Some collectives have been formed voluntarily by the peasants of some areas."

"And now they do not have to be exploited on the free market. They can buy the goods the government monopolies sell at controlled prices, instead of buying the goods the government monopolies sell on the basis of supply and demand."

"Yes. They are much better off that way. The collectives we have in the Pyongyang and Woosan regions have raised crop yields and have been very successful. And they have free medical services, while the farmers who have not joined the collectives have not."

76

"How do those noncollectivized farmers get their medical treatment?"

"They have to pay the doctors and buy the medicine."

"You have not nationalized medicine then?"

"No. That is socialism. We are still in the stage of the Democratic People's Republic. The doctors can have private patients."

"And are the fees controlled?"

"No. There is much more freedom here than you think."

"I was under the impression that Marx condemned this type of freedom."

"That is socialism. We have not yet reached that stage. I must go now."

Out of my window I could see Korean girls searching for sea shells in the shallows of the Tedong Gang. They were too far away for me to tell whether they, too, were beautiful, like their legendary sister whose lover's emeralds turned the water green.

CHAPTER 4

To the Yalu

On August 31, 1950, I was taken back to the civilian-internee camp outside Pyongyang. At once I began to distribute my radio news. Bishop Patrick Burns, the apostolic delegate, who had collapsed after acute bouts of dysentery, managed to stand and ask, "How are the Washington Senators doing?" I told him. He said he felt better after that. Walter Eltringham, a kindly, gigantic engineer of the ECA staff, who had been cut off while in the field and captured, was still bruised from head to foot from the continued beatings he had received during the early days of his capture. "Boy," he said, hearing the news of the preparation for the counterattack, "when we hit them, these guys will feel so low they'll be able to sit on a cigarette card and swing their legs."

The most charming reaction to the B.B.C. news I relayed was among the diplomatic corps. Stealing paper from the guard's desk and writing with homemade instruments, the French diplomats produced a card written in exquisite copperplate, complimenting Captain Vyvyan

78

Holt (the interned British Minister) on the news of the Princess' birth.

Captain Vyvyan Holt, his vice-consul, George Blake; and his pro-consul, Norman Owen—together with Commissioner Lord of the Salvation Army and Father Charles Hunt, who had taken refuge in the Legation in Seoul—were arrested on July 2, 1950 by the North Koreans. During the first hours of Communist rule, some civilians in ragged clothes broke into the Legation compound, flashing their guns at everyone, and demanded the Legation cars. They said they were going to bring them back.

Captain Holt, ignoring the menacing gestures of his uninvited guests, protested through Commissioner Lord, who acted as interpreter.

The next day, a Communist official came and demanded that the Union Jack be lowered. He said that as the Legation stood on high ground, everyone could see the flag and that might cause disturbances. As no member of the Legation staff made any attempt to obey his orders, the Communist official himself lowered the Union Jack, which he folded and handed to Blake before politely taking his leave.

Tanks were still running around the city, firing bursts from their machine guns. Bands of drunken Communists roamed the streets. Others—the Legation servants reported—were searching houses for hidden stocks of rice. Blake and Owen, who had already burned all ciphers,

79

codes, and other confidential material, were busy pouring down the drain the contents of the Legation cellar, lest these be found by some Communists, who might then get even more drunk and decide to shoot up everybody.

Meanwhile, Captain Holt was sitting in his lounge with Commissioner Lord. It was late at night and they sat in darkness, for there was no electricity. Suddenly they heard the noise of a window opening, then shutting.

"Who is that?" asked Commissioner Lord in Korean.

There was the click of a rifle bolt. Then a voice, apparently coming from the floor, said, "Who is that?"

"We are British people. Who are you?"

The answer came after a short silence. "I am a South Korean policeman, hiding from the Communists. You must hide me."

"We cannot hide you here. We, too, are in danger from the Communists. Communist officials come here all the time. You must go."

There were alarming sounds of a rifle being handled, then: "If you try to give me away to the Communist officials I will shoot you."

"We will not give you away, but you are not safe here. If they find you here it will be worse for you and for us."

There was a very long silence, broken finally by the Commissioner.

"Are you still here?" he asked.

"Yes," said the voice from the floor, "but I am going."

In the morning it was found that he had gone but left

behind his uniform and rifle. These were thrown out of the compound, and the waiting was resumed.

By July 2 the people in the compound already knew that Britain had agreed to send forces against the North Koreans. For the five Britons in Communist-held Seoul, this was not a comfortable thought. Still, there was always diplomatic status, and they tried not to think of what might happen—after all, they could not have left. The Legation staff had had no authority to leave its post. Commissioner Lord and Father Hunt could not have gone, leaving their Korean followers alone. Other missionaries had done that before Japan came into World War II, and their departure had been a heavy spiritual blow for the native Christians.

In the evening, just before dinner, the Legation cars drove up before the gates.

"Ah," said Blake, "perhaps they're bringing our cars back as they promised."

In spite of Captain Holt's protests, he and his staff and the two missionaries were driven away in the cars to the central police station.

The official supervising the arrest assured them that they did not need to take any provisions or clothes along as they were only going away for twenty minutes. They had to wait eight hours without a meal, without being told why they had been arrested.

Then a young major came in. He said he wanted to take down some particulars. With him there was an interpreter

81

who assured the prisoners he was not a Communist but had just been brought along to help. The question, it seems, was to establish the identity of the Legation staff. Captain Holt said that in his strong room he had the King's commission, and he was driven back to his house to retrieve that document. When he arrived, he saw that the sack had already begun. North Korean policemen were carrying out documents and clothes. He made another protest there and then. His escort said the matter would be reported to the competent authorities. Back in the police station, the interrogations continued.

George Blake was sitting across the table from the interpreter, who was taking detailed notes on the antecedents of the vice-consul's maternal grandmother when a bullet came up through the floor, through the table, and shattered the inkwell, splattering the two men with ink. The interpreter was very annoyed.

"These boys, they get drunk easily," he said. The interrogation finished, the young major offered his camp bed to Captain Holt, and the other four went on sitting in their chairs. Somebody brought them each a bowl of boiled barley.

At the other end of the room, two South Korean policemen were being interrogated. It appeared that during the earlier part of the interrogation they had tried to kill themselves by jumping from the second-floor windows. Their questioners had brought them back, bleeding, with broken limbs, their faces completely misshapen by bruises, and still the interrogation went on.

The man in whose office all this was taking place was signing death warrants. Commissioner Lord told me of a conversation he overheard between the one who signed and another official.

"When will these men be shot?"

"We killed them yesterday."

"But I had not signed the orders yet."

"You were too busy."

"Don't let it happen again."

The man who signed the death warrants was only a lieutenant.

The little major in charge of the British prisoners got up during the night and announced that it was time to leave for Pyongyang.

Captain Holt protested that the treatment meted out to him and his staff was contrary to international practice, and demanded that he should be allowed to communicate with his Government. He complained about the conditions in which he was kept, and about the sacking of the Legation. In spite of his protest, he was obliged to board a truck bound for Pyongyang. With Captain Holt, his staff, and the two missionaries, there were also a White Russian diver who had worked for ECA, and two Americans, Louis Dans, assistant manager of the Traders Exchange in Seoul, and Walter Eltringham, the ECA coal-mine expert.

During the drive, the little major accidentally shot a small
village boy in the leg while practicing with his newly issued Russian pistol; then he drove the boy to a hospital.

In Pyongyang, the five Britons, the two Americans, and
the White Russian were taken to the dilapidated school
building which they initiated as the foreign civilian internee camp in North Korea. The White Russian diver was
removed by the authorities soon after their arrival and was
never seen again, and the seven western internees remained on their own until the middle of July, when the
French diplomats joined them, together with missionaries
and civilians of other nationalities.

The Communists had been in Seoul a full two weeks before they arrested the staff of the French Legation—
Georges Perruche, the consul-general; Jean Meadmore,
the vice-consul; Martel, the chancellor—and those Europeans who had taken refuge in the compound. The people
under Georges Perruche's protection included Mrs. Lottie
Gliese, a citizen of East Berlin, and Matti, the Swiss
manager of the Chosun Hotel—both neutrals.

All these people were taken to the Seoul police station,
where they met the arrested Catholic missionaries and
Bishop Patrick Burns and were herded into a large hall
with South Korean political prisoners. There was one meal
of barley a day, only one occasion daily for going to the
lavatory, and constant screaming abuse from the guards.
The temperature was over 100 degrees. The hall was not

ventilated and disease set in—mainly dysentery—from the unclean food and the unboiled water.

Perruche, irresistible even to Communist guards, managed to persuade them to let him collect some clothes and equipment from his house in a suitcase. Thus, he was practically the only internee with any sort of equipment, but since he distributed it all among the rest, he was soon as denuded as the others. Between intervals of cajoling the guards and trying to alleviate the fate of their fellow internees, Perruche and Meadmore, through their imperturbable interpreter, Martel, faced interrogator after interrogator, and started on what became practically their specialty—"disintoxicating Asiatic minds drunk with Marx," as they put it.

Before they left for Pyongyang, the French were kept at a railway siding in a sealed cattle car, packed with so many people that no one could stretch. Only squatting was possible. In that cattle car took place Perruche's first celebration of the Fourteenth of July as "déchargé d'affaires"—the title he adopted after his arrest. With the help of some bottles of Burgundy—part of the "equipment" he had packed in his suitcase—Perruche got even the doomed South Korean political prisoners into something approaching a celebration mood. Morale had to be kept up, and the health of M. Vincent Auriol, President of the French Republic, was duly drunk in good French wine.

There were raids by United Nations planes, and strafing

85

of the trains in the station. The explosions shook the car. The South Korean political prisoners wailed, but the French kept up their spirits and never lost the optimism which had motivated one of them—an unmarried one—to take contraceptives along into captivity.

"On ne sait jamais, mon cher," he said, explaining his action with a Gallic shrug, *"on ne sait jamais."*

Then they arrived at the internee camp in Pyongyang, where they proceeded to organize themselves, started a Belotte school which produced discussions that wandered wittily from their original topic to everything under the sun, and kept the rest of the internees listening expectantly for the next instalment.

On September 5, 1950, at six in the evening of an extremely rainy day, a short, fat little colonel, whom we called the Panjandrum, came and took us away in trucks.

We were first driven to the Pyongyang jail, where we stayed for an hour, then to the station. After squatting in the rain for an hour we boarded a train, which was in complete darkness and seemed to be full of Americans: Brooklynese, Texas drawls, and the soft accents of New England mingled in voicing imprecations about the guards. The train rolled intermittently through the night. In the morning we left it and walked up the nearby hills to take shelter from United Nations planes.

Here we got our first glimpse of our American prisoner companions. They were indescribably dirty. They said they had not washed since their capture. After the march from the front, during which they had had experiences corresponding to mine, they were put in a large school near Pyongyang. There they were not treated brutally and were fed bread twice a day, rice and dried fish once a day, meat three times a week, apples, and sugar. But they had not been able to wash, and were crawling with lice. A large proportion of them had no shoes. They wore light-weight summer fatigues. They were traveling packed tight in open coal cars. Some had been given old cotton quilts, but even they were bitterly cold during the journey through the North Korean September days.

Then the sick appeared. Thinner even than their "healthy" companions, they walked like figures in a slow-motion film, helped along by their own medical orderlies and by Korean nurses. They were given medical treatment during the day and some extra food, which most of them could not keep down. One of them, a Roman Catholic, died, and Monsignor Quinlan put up a tremendous and finally victorious fight with the commandant for permission to hold a burial service. Another died while the grave was being dug. The two G.I.'s were buried in a common grave at the small village of Maran. A Christian villager, whispering, promised that he would tend the graves.

We walked back to the train at dusk to find it had been strafed by United Nations planes. The next day the train commandant made an odd little speech to the civilian internees. He told us that it had been very troublesome capturing us. Why had we stayed behind to be captured? There had been no policy then, but now there was. We were to be treated kindly. We—the special group of diplomats and journalists—were to have sleeper accommodations. They were verminous, but better than the open coal cars in which most of the G.I.'s traveled, and in which —it must be said—the Korean civilian passengers traveled also.

We reached our destination, Manpo, the frontier town of the Central Korea-Manchuria railway line, on September 11, 1950. There we were accommodated in what had been the quarantine quarters.

Judging by the standards of the neighboring villagers, we were living in the lap of luxury, with an egg a day, meat three times a week, sugar, oil. In the afternoon we could bathe in the river and sit for as long as we liked on the sunny beach. We were allowed to go to town shopping with what money the diplomats managed to get out of the guards in exchange for their watches.

Dr. Kim Pyong Gu visited us daily, administered diarrhea pills, and sang "You came, I was alone, I should have known, you were temptation, and I . . ." to a sixteen-year-old White Russian girl named Sagida. He told us that he was losing two or three G.I.'s every day from pneumonia, because he had no sulfapyridine, no blankets, no clothes, and the prisoner-of-war barracks could not be heated until October 1. He also complained that many of the deaths were due to the fact that some of the G.I.'s did not seem anxious to live. His statements were later corroborated by American prisoners of war with whom I talked.

During our stay in Manpo, two American G.I.'s attempted to escape. They were caught three days later. When I talked to them later they assured me they had not been in any way brutalized. The only punishment meted out to them was deprivation of tobacco for a week.

At the well where we got our water, a fifteen-year-old Korean boy, a Presbyterian, daily handed us a written summary of the United Nations Korean broadcast. Thus we learned of the landings at Inchon, and knew that the United Nations forces had invaded North Korea. This information service, organized by Commissioner Herbert Lord of the Salvation Army, went undetected by our guards. Day by day we heard of the advances made by those we hoped were to be our liberators. Sweepstakes were started. Plans were made about freedom, about the gifts that we would buy for our relatives. That first telegram was mentally written and rewritten. And at night we stayed up, anxiously counting the trains rumbling over the international bridge between Korea and China. We could not see them, we could only hear them. Were they coming in or going out? By day we could see, high up in the sky, planes with Western markings. Even when they were miles inside Korean territory, Chinese batteries fired at the United Nations planes.

On October 8, under heavy rain, we were told to move,

taking with us our cast-iron cooking pots and all our stores. A Mother Superior of the Carmelites, suffering from a recurrence of tuberculosis and unable to walk, was carried on a homemade stretcher. There were three false starts. We got thoroughly wet, and finally left on the ninth for our next camp, at Kosang Djin, having been unable to cook during the delay because the kitchen had been dismantled.

At our new place, fifteen miles down the Yalu River from Manpo, we were settled in a schoolhouse, and the Korean major in charge of the camp obviously tried, with the means at his disposal, to give us a good time. One day he came, gathered us around, and looking very solemn, made an almost apologetic speech.

"We are," he said, "a very small nation, very poor. We have been slaves of the Japanese for fifty years. After 1945 we started an independent life. You do not like our methods. You are anti-Communists. But you must try to understand us. We were centuries behind. We could not wait for normal development. We had to go faster. I have tried, on orders from my Government, to treat you well. Some of you had a bad time at the beginning, we know. This was not what our Government wanted. Mistakes are made. You will be going to your homes. You will be in your rich countries, which we have not attacked. You must remember that we have tried to do our best."

We thought, having heard the major's speech, that liberation was near.

90

"Any time now, any time now," said Father Cadars, a peppery little French priest of seventy-two, who, after forty years in the Church, still showed that once he had been an artillery captain.

Father Cadars had been in Taejon when the Communists captured the town. He told me that just before the Americans retreated from the town, South Korean police brought 1,700 men, loaded layer upon layer in trucks, into a forest clearing near his church. These prisoners were taken out and ordered to dig long trenches. Father Cadars watched. Some American officers, Cadars said, were also watching. When a certain amount of digging had been completed, South Korean policemen shot half the prisoners in the back of the neck. The other half were ordered to bury the dead. Horrified, Father Cadars had approached the South Korean officer in command.

"Why are these men being shot?"

"Because they are Communist guerrillas who rebelled in the Taejon jail."

"Have you tried them?"

"Grandfather, it is better for you that you should not know too much about this."

And Father Cadars was roughly pushed aside. Kneeling behind a bush, he prayed for those who were being killed, the group being methodically diminished by half each time, the surviving half being made to bury the dead before their own turn came.

Weeks before I was told this story, while I was still in

91

the Japanese villa in Pyongyang where I had been pressed to prove that I was not a spy, I had been visited by Alan Winnington, correspondent of the London *Daily Worker.* He did not come to interrogate me, to indoctrinate me, or even to interview me. He came to be pleasant to a fellow journalist; he brought gifts. He did not even talk of the Korean war, except for one thing. He told me that near Taejon a mass grave had been discovered in which hundreds of South Korean Communists had been buried after being shot without trial. He said this had been done in the presence of American officers. I told him I did not believe his story. I did not—until Father Cadars repeated it to me.

Father Cadars was never to know liberation. Nor were we in October, 1950. Late in the month we heard the terrible news that the Chinese had come into the war. Our thoughts were with our families at home. We were afraid for them because we thought that the third world war was about to start. Meanwhile, the United Nations forces were still advancing. We got conflicting, puzzling snatches of news from well-disposed civilians, from guards who begged us to protect them if our troops reached the Yalu. They all—we know now—exaggerated the successes of our troops, and raised our hopes too high.

As our quarters were needed for the incoming Chinese, we were marched—internees and P.O.W.'s alike—over mountain paths to a remote mining hamlet, Chui Am Nee, where we experienced a strange, tantalizing interlude.

We were put in derelict houses. It was already freezing cold. Searching in fetid, open sewers, the barefooted Carmelites looked for fuel. Their tubercular Mother Superior needed warmth. The kindly major was not there. Over the hills came small groups of ragged North Korean soldiers, battle-weary, wounded, dispirited, and hostile. A Communist quartermaster captain opened the village warehouse and told the G.I.'s to take what they wanted. There were old fur bonnets and gloves. There was also some flour. We had our first meal in twenty-four hours.

Then the quartermaster disappeared. No one seemed to be in charge. Stragglers still came from the south going north. This, we told ourselves, was the debacle. Some talked of organizing a committee to run things now we had been left alone. Others talked of taking over the village. There were villagers who hoped we would do so. Lying in our cold, verminous, low-ceilinged rooms, or delousing by the side of the open sewers, we assured one another that these were the last days of hunger, that over the hills, after the stragglers, would soon come our own troops; that the Communists fleeing into Manchuria had brought us to this out-of-the-way valley so that we would be liberated without risking getting involved in the actual fighting. "Oh yes," said the villagers, "three more days, perhaps four, and they'll be here."

We were very hungry, very cold, but very happy.

One night, three of us decided to escape and go towards the armed forces to bring help. We met near one of our huts, ready to go, our feet bound in rags, with a stick each, and a compass that somebody had managed to bring along. We were ready to go, but where? Each of us had a favorite itinerary. We argued in whispers which gradually grew louder. The other occupants of the hut shouted angrily that we should keep quiet. Unable to sleep because of our continuing argument, they listened, became interested, and finally came out. They formed a circle around us, lit a small fire and joined in the discussion, which grew louder and woke the occupants of the next hut. They, too, joined in. This brought the next hut out. We stood in the middle, silenced now by our elders, who had congregated and were discussing our fate.

There were two schools of thought: one that it was wrong of us to attempt an escape because those remaining behind would be victimized, and the other that we should attempt the escape, as we were young and active, to bring help in the form of parachutists. Misinformed as we were by the villagers, we thought help was just around the corner; therefore the second school prevailed. Yes, we should attempt the escape, but should we do it alone, or should we try to take along one of the South Korean politicians interned with our group? Would one of them be ready to come? Why not ask them?

The seven South Korean politicians were alerted. They squatted on their heels near the small fire, rocking gently back and forth. This was a matter for grave decision. They were flattered at being consulted, and they were going to

94

make the most of this occasion. They made long speeches, with simultaneous whispered translations by those who understood Korean. They considered the various routes and the chances of success. The chances would be greater if one of them were to join us, but if he were caught he would surely be killed. On the other hand, should he manage to bring us through, he would be a great hero and would be made much of by the Americans. That was a distinction worth considering. It was considered.

Then one of the politicians suggested that before making any decisions it was preferable to get the latest bulletin. There was a man in the village who had a brother who was a carpenter working for the army some miles away and often overheard information. The brother of the carpenter would know if anybody would. Trained diplomats and journalists, high dignitaries of various denominations, a former member of the South Korean Government, all waited to hear from the carpenter's brother. This man came himself and squatted near the small fire. Elaborate greetings were exchanged, and every word became longer as honorific endings were tacked on to it—for the carpenter's brother was an important man and had to be flattered. He, too, pondered over the various problems and finally gave his advice. Yes, the escape should be tried. Help was just around the corner. He was thanked elaborately and departed, leaving the council to decide.

I don't know who noticed him first. There, sitting among us, was a North Korean policeman who, during these few days when we felt abandoned by the authorities, had kept a sort of vague watch over us. He appeared extremely interested in the discussion, and although he had his tommy-gun at the ready, he did not really look hostile.

Somebody giggled, then we all laughed, except the Korean politicians, who did not know we were laughing at ourselves and thought we were laughing at them. In stately procession they went back to their hut, immensely dignified and immensely hurt.

The senior member of our group of "Korean gentlemen" —as they called themselves—was Kim Hyo Suk, who had been Syngman Rhee's Minister of the Interior shortly before the Communist invasion. He had run the South Korean security forces when the guerrilla campaigns were at their height in the South. He had signed the orders for the ferocious reprisals with which the Reds had been fought. It was under his administration that the scorched-earth policy had been adopted—whole areas destroyed—to keep the guerrillas from getting supplies. The Communists caught him hiding as a peasant in the country near Seoul. They had so much against him that he was helpless in their hands. Under constant pressure, he produced the major document in the Blue Book issued by the North Korean Government in September, 1950, to prove that it was the South which had started the war. Kim Hyo Suk, impassive and cynical though he was, flinched every time he was approached by a Communist official, and when taken away for an interrogation he went as if going to his death. He gave the impression of being ready to say or write anything—and it is not possible to blame him. He asked me once not to believe everything I was told he had written, and to "understand."

Besides the ex-Minister, we had with us a Mr. Chaigh, who had been the secretary of the big landowners' party; a Japanese-trained professor who spoke good English and whom we called Big Mr. Pak, to differentiate him from Small Mr. Pak, a farmer; and Messrs. Chang and Lee, both of whom claimed to be anti-Japanese resistance leaders. All these were Members of the South Korean Parliament. But the greatest personality of the group was not. He was the only one of the seven who had failed to get elected in May, 1950, in spite of the fact that his brothelkeeper mistress had spent millions of inflated *won* to plaster the streets of Keson with the bearded likeness of her lover. Having lost the election, Moon Hak Pong decided he no longer needed to look quite so dignified and old. He shaved his beard, and formed a party composed of vigorous young men, ready and eager to undertake any kind of job. It was not a big party, and he told me he could easily finance it with the income from his mistress' brothel and with the fees he received from "personages in high places" for "odd jobs" he performed from time to time. Besides these fees, he received contracts and governmental patronage. In exchange, one could depend on Moon Hak Pong whenever unpleasant critics had to be silenced, obstreperous Members of Parliament recalled to order, or

97

incriminating evidence suppressed. So claimed Moon Hak Pong, a typical Far Eastern comprador—amoral, tough, courageous, treacherous, superstitious, and very pleased with himself.

In moments of stress, he would stand at attention with his hands pressed to his chest, facing the sun, looking straight into the fiery ball. Thus strengthened by contemplation, he would walk up and down alone for a while.

After one such session, he said to me, "You will write about me—I am great man. Perhaps some day you understand. Perhaps some day I can tell you. Now I cannot. Later, perhaps, I give you great news. You are newsman, yes? You want great news, no?" And without waiting for an answer, pursing his eyelids till they were mere wrinkles, he walked away—this Sumo wrestler who tried hard to look like a Buddha.

Moon Hak Pong had a thirst for leadership. By chicanery, flattery, lies, small services, and threats, he had emerged as the leader of the civilian internees. There were seventy of us. Many members of the group were people accustomed to authority, people who resented Mr. Moon's leadership—after he had been appointed headman by the kindly major who administered us at Kosang Djin. Yet at Chui Am Nee, where we were left to administer our own affairs and the major was not there to back Mr. Moon's authority, the latter remained in the saddle, much to the annoyance of many, and there were some whites who resented the authority of a "yellow man."

The kindly major reappeared on October 26, 1950, and ordered us to move. He would not say where we were going, and he would not answer questions. Then he left us. The G.I.'s went ahead. Those who were too sick were left behind. We do not know what happened to them. The civilian internees were under the charge of the quartermaster captain who had opened up the Chui Am Nee warehouse to the G.I.'s.

Mr. Moon was in cahoots with the quartermaster captain. They held frequent conferences that were very much resented by the other six Korean politicians and—it must be said—by those among us who aspired to leadership. Big Mr. Pak, the intellectual, was always ready to express his contempt for "that bad man, Mr. Moon": "He is nobody. He has no education. He has no moral values. He does not even speak good English."

Mr. Moon did not speak good English. His vocabulary was very limited, but he used it so impressively that he was always employed as the official interpreter. What this gangster in his middle thirties did not understand, when interpreting, he tried to guess by looking at our faces, and then, glibly, he gave his version in Korean—the version that suited his purpose best.

"He does not say what you said," Big Mr. Pak would hiss, his five fellow Members of Parliament, their hands tucked inside their sleeves, indignantly assenting. "He does not understand what you say. He just says what he thinks best for him."

99

"Even if he understood," remarked Captain Holt, "he would still say what he thought best for him."

All this aloud, in the presence of Mr. Moon, who screwed up his eyes and looked inscrutable, and who later —we all knew—would take revenge on Big Mr. Pak. Meanwhile, he was the unmistakable leader, relishing to the full the privilege of talking in private with the heads of the diplomatic missions, familiarly holding the arm of His Majesty's Minister or of the French chargé d'affaires, and triumphantly conscious of the murderous looks the other six Koreans leveled at him.

Mr. Moon's colleagues had not always confined their hostile reactions to murderous looks. Once, in Kosang Djin, they had taken the kitchen knives and rushed at Moon Hak Pong. That was inside their room, and the door was closed. Outside, we listened breathlessly to the gasps, the sounds of blows, the noises of scuffle. Then there was a long silence, followed by speeches. Kim Hyo Suk spoke first, then Big Mr. Pak. Mr. Chang made a short but hysterical speech. Mr. Chaigh was agitated and stuttered. Mr. Lee sounded important. Little Mr. Pak did not say much. Then there was silence again. What had happened to Mr. Moon? Why could we not hear his voice? When he spoke at last, we almost breathed a sigh of relief. Mr. Moon had about him the exotic aura of the Far Eastern brigands, and lent a touch of color to our gray, sordid existence. He spoke long, then came out. On his face there was something like a smile. Inside the room, the quarrel was going on, the other six were at it hard. Mr. Moon had never read Julius Caesar or Niccolò Machiavelli, but he knew their business. Looking straight ahead, he went to the kitchen and returned the knives his colleagues had borrowed for their thwarted assault.

Disappointed because the Communists had not accepted him into their ranks, and convinced that he had underestimated the Americans in July, 1950, Mr. Moon was ready by the end of October to try his luck once more with the Western world. He wanted to return to political life in South Korea as the man who had served the civilian internees in general and the diplomats in particular. This, he felt sure, would be widely publicized: had he not with him two journalists representing international news organizations?

To this end, he had convinced the quartermaster captain that all was up with the Communists. We suspected that Mr. Moon, speaking for the group, had promised much to this North Korean officer. That is why, after we left Chui Am Nee, the quartermaster captain said, "Walk slowly, walk very slowly." We marched at less than a mile an hour. The quartermaster captain asked me to go to the front and to walk even more slowly. We nearly marked time. We were going back to Kosang Djin. During the day we negotiated a snow-covered pass, and reached a farmhouse a quarter of the distance to our destination.

"We shall rest here for some time," said the quartermaster captain. "You must be tired." He produced carrots and beans, and fed us.

That night, Moon Hak Pong called some of us together.

"I," he said, "think we must do something. I think perhaps we must go. I think it very important Captain Holt and Mr. Perruche must go, and others together. Also the journalists must go. You make ready. I will see guide soon. I will tell you. Be ready."

We felt almost sick with excitement. Stragglers were still coming over the hills, and the peasants kept saying: "Any day now."

Someone had started the story that we were being taken to the area in which the Communists would make their last stand before crossing into China. In this redout, the story went, we would be treated very badly, and made to trail along behind the retreating remnants of the routed Red Army. In this redout we would all be killed before the American troops reached us. According to this story, the only hope left for us was parachute rescue, and someone had to warn the Americans to come and save us. So, some of us had to escape to tell the outside world of our plight. Mr. Moon's plan, whatever its motives, fell in with ours.

That first night at the farmhouse, between Chui Am Nee and Kosang Djin, those of us who were members of the escape party were too excited to sleep. We waited for Mr. Moon to give us the signal, but nothing happened all night. In the morning, the quartermaster captain, a sergeant, and a guard played a sort of checkers game with Mr. Moon. When that was over, Mr. Moon contemplated the Sun, turning a deaf ear to all our questions. Refreshed by his exercise, he called some of us together, assured us all was well and said he had the guide he had promised, only we had not started during the previous night because there was one thing he had to do first. Then he borrowed Mr. Perruche's pack of cards and disappeared in the direction of some bushes. Making a large detour so that he would not notice me, I crawled close to where he was. Opposite him sat a White Russian woman belonging to our group. She was laying the cards down in rows on a piece of cloth.

"This," she said, pointing, "shows you are going to go on a long journey. And this shows much money at the end of the journey. And there are many women waiting for you."

"I go alone, yes?"

The White Russian woman looked at Mr. Moon, trying to guess the answer he wanted.

"You go alone," she said. Then, seeing the disappointment on his face, she quickly added, "I mean you go alone to the women, but you do not go alone on the journey. You go with other people."

"At the end of journey, do I have much honor?"

"Oh yes," said the Russian woman. "Here, you can see what honor. There is the king and he has you—you are the jack—on his right hand, and here are the women. And the other jacks are those who go with you on the journey."

"Is this a good day for me?"

"I must lay the cards again for that," said the Russian woman, shuffling the pack. "Cut, please. Oh yes, see all the red diamonds. It is a very good day."

"Thank you," said Moon Hak Pong, rising and giving her a handful of tobacco which he must have stolen. "Today I make important thing. You see. I go."

A few minutes later, he had another conference with the quartermaster captain, who then expressed a desire to communicate with the diplomats and journalists.

"Those of you who are fit," the captain said, "why do you not go south? Take a walk. Find out about the situation. And perhaps you can come and report to me. See how the sick are in Chui Am Nee. If you don't come back, I shall understand. My sergeant and one guard want to come with you. If you meet any of your important friends, tell them about me. Remember I've been good to you. Perhaps, if you meet your important friends, you can tell them about the fate of the others who cannot walk with you because they are not young. Perhaps something can be done for them."

Astonished, we set off south in the company of a sergeant who carried a tommygun and a soldier with a rifle. They were friendly. Through the Japanese speakers among us they assured us that they personally had always been against any idea of ill-treating us. Would we please remember that if we met important friends?

We passed a North Korean official who, because we were escorted, never questioned our right to be where we were. At the top of a second mountain pass, a Korean policeman stopped our sergeant and they had a long conversation together. Then the sergeant said, "We must go back."

"Why?"

"The Chinese have won a great victory. They now hold the whole road. It is very difficult to go south. It is better for me to stay with my people. The great Chinese nation is helping us. We will have a good life when we win."

Mr. Moon took the sergeant and the guard aside. He produced tobacco and some newspaper. Cigarettes were rolled. We watched. The palaver lasted a long time. Then Mr. Moon walked over to us.

"He thinks the Chinese are going to win. And he thinks that when we go to our side we will forget him, that we will not do anything for him."

"Tell him we promise solemnly to look after him."

Mr. Moon transmitted the message to the sergeant.

"He says what are we going to do for him?"

That little Korean sergeant was offered a British Council scholarship, a guarantee of free studies at the Sorbonne, large sums of money. For a time he wavered. Could his friend also have a scholarship? Of course he could. All the time he kept his tommygun pointing towards us, the safety catch off. Finally he decided that he was not prepared to take the risk of passing through the Chinese lines. We went back, deeply depressed, feeling that we had perhaps been very close to freedom.

105

Back at the farmhouse we were met by the quarter-master captain, who solemnly thanked us for all our efforts. He invited me, as representative of the group, to eat with him. He had managed to get some dried fish, not enough for everybody, but he would be delighted if I joined him.

Mr. Moon acted as interpreter at that dinner. He told me the captain felt very sorry at the terrible things that were going to happen to us. Suddenly I felt my appetite going. Later that day, the march was resumed. We were some fifteen miles from Manpo, and it took us three days to get there. Mr. Moon, on behalf of the captain, told us to walk slowly, more slowly.

The other Koreans rebelled against the directive of their hated compatriot. They decided to walk faster. Mr. Moon shook his head sadly and reported them to the quarter-master captain, who barked something, and the six Members of the South Korean Parliament fell back into line.

"They no understand," said Mr. Moon. "They have small minds, not like me."

He had found an enormous old straw hat somewhere, and a blanket which he wore like a serape. Walking beside the column, he reminded me of Wallace Beery playing the role of Pancho Villa, the Mexican revolutionary general.

"I," he said, "am great man."

He was.

We spent the nights in Presbyterian churches along the route, and fed on boiled corn once a day.

On the road, Chinese soldiers passed us. There were

signboards with directions for the "Chinese People's Army." They were not calling themselves volunteers.

Those, perhaps, were our worst moments. The Chinese were pouring in by the thousands, complete with artillery, automatic rifles, and brand-new Molotov trucks. Korean stragglers, wounded, their clothes torn, screamed insults as we passed and worked their bolts threateningly at us. Was this the third world war? Were our people already being bombed? Would we ever be free again?

CHAPTER 5

Death March

ON THE night of October 30, we reached Manpo. We stopped by a burned house near a saw mill. It was already freezing hard. We huddled around a straw fire, trying to warm ourselves. The children, cold and hungry, were crying, and already, Dr. Kisch told us, the Carmelite Mother Superior was dying. Half a mile away the G.I.'s were camping in an open field. During the night a Korean officer came and kicked out our fire.

Then Mr. Moon disappeared. He came back an hour later, looking extremely agitated. In the morning, he said, we would change hands, the prison warders would take over. He squatted like a Buddha.

"This is the end," he said.

Headed by Big Mr. Pak, the other Koreans came to bid us good-by. In the morning, they said, we would be separated and they would be shot. Big Mr. Pak wept a little. We tried to console him.

George Blake, the British vice-consul, made an attempt to escape that night. He walked south, over one hill and

then another, until he heard a bolt clicking and a voice
screaming something at him in Korean. He raised his arms
above his head, and was escorted by his captor to a farm,
where a number of Korean officers interviewed him in Russian.

Why was he escaping? He was not escaping.

What was he doing, then, when he was found? He was
taking a walk.

Why? He had felt cold where the others were sitting.

The Korean officers laughed.

"You are lying," they said. "You were trying to escape.
Don't you realize you cannot possibly escape with your big
nose and your red skin? You must not be silly. Have some
food."

Blake ate pork soup with white rice and was given a
packet of twenty cigarettes. He was told to sleep. With his
characteristic ability to shed worry, he lay on the heated
floor and slept soundly till the morning, when he was
brought back to us. Meanwhile, there had been a roll call,
and Commissioner Lord had lied solidly for fifteen minutes, finally convincing the guard in charge that no one
was missing although there was one less in the group.

Then, just as Mr. Moon had predicted, a group of prison
warders came up to us, headed by a major who said he was
now in charge.

"He's all right," said Blake. "He's the man who caught
me last night. He was not at all angry. He gave me pork
soup and rice."

109

This was the man we later came to call "the Tiger," the man whom Monsignor Quinlan and Father Canavan had already met as governor of the Chunchon jail.

We were lined up and ordered to empty our pockets. We had to surrender all penknives. The old people had to surrender their sticks. Odd bits of straw matting had to be dropped.

"I," said the Tiger, pulling down an epaulette in a gesture we were to know well, "am a major of the People's Army. I am to be obeyed. I have authority to make you obey. You will march to another place now."

We started marching in a long straggly line preceded by the G.I.'s. As we were going through the town of Manpo, a limousine stopped beside us, and two civilians stepped out. They stood there, in their thick overcoats, lined gloves and fur bonnets, impassively watching us pass. One of them was recognized by the diplomats in our group as an old acquaintance—Mr. Kotikov, Russian consul in Peking. Some of the diplomats who were in this march, dressed in summer clothes and torn or nonexistent footwear, obviously ill, had given hospitality to Mr. Kotikov in the recent past, had had long talks with him. He stood there and watched them pass.

We marched nearly through the night, passing the town of Manpo and taking the road to Kangai. We stopped in an open field to sleep. It was very cold. The Mother Superior of the Carmelites was having a hemorrhage. The babies in our extraordinary company were weeping. Yet we slept, because we were exhausted. In the morning our beards were white with frozen breath. In a pile, some distance away, were the naked bodies of G.I.'s who had frozen to death during the night.

I asked why they were naked. Had the clothes been taken away from them after they died?

"Before they died," I was told, "while they were dying. Some of the others wanted them."

The march continued during the day after a meal of boiled corn. The eighty-two-year-old French missionary was being carried by Monsignor Quinlan. Miss Nellie Dyer, an American Methodist missionary, was carrying Sister Mary Clare, an Anglican nun, in her arms. Father Charles Hunt, the Anglican missionary, suffering from gout, was being dragged along by his companions. Commissioner Lord, the column's official interpreter, had tied a rope around the waist of Mme. Funderat, a seventy-year-old White Russian, and was pulling her along. Two White Russian women walked with crying, cold, hungry babies on their backs, holding their other young children by the hand. The children who were not being carried had to trot because the pace was too quick for their gait. Two Carmelite nuns were coughing up blood. They was shod in rough wooden sandals they had made themselves. Norman Owen, pro-consul at the British Legation, Seoul, had as his only footwear Father Hunt's chasuble, divided in two with a half for each foot. The septuagenarian French fathers, obliged to stop because of their dysentery, were egged on

111

by the guards, who fired off their rifles near the old men's ears.

Ahead, the G.I.'s, still in summer fatigues, a large proportion with no shoes, marched in a long, straggly column of threes; soon many were being carried. Frequently the exhausted carriers would drop their charges and we would pass creatures, hard to recognize as human, prostrate on the road. During the morning of November 1, too many dropped out. The Tiger called the American platoon commanders together. Speaking through Commissioner Lord, he said, "No one must drop out. I order you not to allow anyone to drop out." He pulled down his epaulette. "I have authority to make you obey. If you do not, I will punish you with the extreme penalty of military discipline. Even the dead must be carried."

The march was resumed. Before noon men had dropped out of every platoon. The Tiger stopped the column and called the platoon leaders together. A crowd of North Korean soldiers gathered. Speaking through Commissioner Lord, he said, "You have disobeyed my orders. I have authority to punish you. I will now shoot you all."

Commissioner Lord, in his flawless Korean, started pleading for the lives of those young Americans. The Tiger pulled his pistol and put it to the head of Commissioner Lord.

The Commissioner did not stop talking. I do not know what he told the major, but the latter did not shoot; instead, he asked for the officer from whose platoon the greatest number had dropped out. Lieutenant Cordus H. Thornton took three steps forward.

"Why did you let those five men drop out?" asked the Tiger.

"Because, sir, they were dying."

"Why did you not obey my orders and have them carried?"

"Because, sir, that meant condemning the carriers to death from exhaustion."

"You knew I had ordered no one should drop out?"

"Yes, sir."

"In wartime the penalty for disobedience is death. You disobeyed orders. I will kill you. That is what would happen in the American Army also, is it not?"

"In the American Army, sir, there would be a trial."

The Tiger turned to the assembled Korean soldiers. "I have authority to kill him. He has disobeyed orders. What must I do?"

"Kill him," screamed the soldiers, "kill them all."

"You see," said the major to Lieutenant Thornton, "you have had your trial, a People's Trial, People's Justice. Now I will kill you."

"In Texas," said Thornton, a tone of contempt in his voice, "we call that lynching, not justice."

Commissioner Lord, with tears running down his cheeks, fell on his knees before the Tiger, begging for Thornton's life. The Tiger put his pistol to the Commissioner's head.

113

"Commissioner," said Thornton, "there's no sense in two of us dying. The others need you."

Someone pulled the Commissioner away.

"Tell him," said the Tiger, pointing to Thornton, "he must turn about."

Lieutenant Cordus H. Thornton was on parade. His shoulders squared, head up, chin in, arms firmly at his sides, he about-faced as one does during drill. The Tiger took a handkerchief and bound Lieutenant Thornton's eyes. Then with his pistol he shot him in the back of the neck. A tall, blond sergeant jumped forward and caught his officer's body before it touched the ground. Tenderly, as if carrying a child, the sergeant took the lieutenant's body to the ditch. We marched on.

That night, the Tiger made a speech and told us that those who had dropped out were being cared for in the People's Hospitals. Five minutes later, he called Commissioner Lord to one side and made him sign a certificate that those who had dropped out had died of heart failure. That night more G.I.'s froze to death. In the morning, before the march was resumed, the Tiger said that those who could not walk were to drop out. He said they would be taken to the People's Hospital. Eighteen exhausted soldiers could not walk. Speaking to the village headman in Korean, in the presence of Commissioner Lord, the Tiger said, "As soon as we are gone, bury them without mounds."

The next day we were told to stop carrying Mother

Superior Beatrice, aged seventy-seven, of the Order of St. Paul. She had devoted all her life to Korean orphans. We were told she would be taken to the People's Hospital. A few minutes later there was a shot. That night Commissioner Lord, a pistol at his head, wrote Mother Beatrice's death certificate: "from heart failure."

The nights were almost worse than the days. The first two were spent in the open. On the third night, the seventy civilian internees were put in a room where each person had a space of three feet by eighteen inches. It was my turn to order sleeping arangements. The heads of families demanded extra space for their wives and sick children. They had to be refused, and driven to desperation by the torture of seeing their loved ones brutalized, they became violent. We were packed so tightly that it was impossible, except for those nearest the door, to get out. And those suffering from dysentery could not wait. We crouched, not sleeping, but stupefied by the fatigue, the memories of the day, the cold, the stench, and the pain in our sick bodies. Like an eerie theme song, the shrill wail of the hungry, sick children hung in the air.

The next night, twenty-seven of us were put in a room nine feet by nine. There was no window, and a sympathetic guard had lit the fire which heated the floor. Then he was replaced by another guard, who was not sympathetic and would not let us open the door. The heat, the smell of dysentery, became intolerable. Our vermin, excited by the rise in temperature, seemed to run amok.

115

"Philip, my son," said Bishop Patrick Burns, the apostolic delegate, his voice hardly audible, "the Koreans are crushing me to death against the wall. Please help me."

Messrs. Chaigh, Chang, Lee, and Pak, to make more space for themselves, were pressing Bishop Burns against the wall. Some of us spent the rest of the night trying to keep the Koreans from crushing Bishop Burns. That night, one of the missionaries temporarily went out of his mind.

On November 4, we crossed a mountain pass in a bitter blizzard. More and more G.I.'s were dropping out. They lay by the side of the road, mutely looking at the departing column. A young, red-headed kid, who could still walk, was trying, weeping, to carry a dying friend. A guard kicked him on. He stumbled off, sobbing. We heard many shots. At one point in the serpentine windings of the road, stopping because of dysentery, I looked down to the lower bend. The Tiger was pushing one of the dying with his foot into the ditch. When the G.I. was completely off the road, the Tiger shot him. I saw two more killed this way on the lower bend of the road before the guard kicked me on.

We marched on, arriving at our destination, Chung Kang Djin, on November 8, 1950, having left behind a hundred dead, buried without mounds in "People's Hospitals."

The moment we arrived, the Tiger said that because of the recalcitrant attitude shown by all during the march, he was going to tighten discipline, and immediately there was half an hour of physical-training exercises.

At seven the next morning the internees were ordered out for more exercise. Everyone had to leave the freezing rooms of this dilapidated Japanese-built school and go out into the courtyard, bounded on three sides by a ramshackle fence. Guards were standing every few yards along the fence, their tommyguns at the ready. Father Paul Villemot, eighty-two, was dying. The Commissioner told the Tiger the old man could not stand. "You," said the Tiger, cocking his pistol and placing it on the Commissioner's temple, "are not obeying orders."

Walter Eltringham and Monsignor Quinlan lifted Father Villemot and carried him out into the courtyard to do physical training. The Tiger took his pistol away from Commissioner Lord's head. That afternoon, Father Villemot died in the country he had refused to leave on retirement. Sister Mary Clare, the Anglican nun, was already dead. The other old priests were dying. Father Jules Gombert, aged seventy-four and a shadow of his former merry-eyed Father-Christmas self, told me, "I know I am sinning, but I want to die, Monsieur Philip. I am giving the poor sisters so much trouble, and I am so disgusting, so smelly, so covered with lice that I cannot bear it. The good Lord is making me weaker. I do hope you will survive, my son." The old man, putting his arms around my neck, wept. The next morning I had to help carry him out for physical training. In the afternoon he died. Monsignor Quinlan, gaunt, his feet misshapen by beri-beri and frostbite stretching his Korean rubber slippers, buried them all, standing in the biting wind, his thin summerweight soutane with the red piping blown about him, still smiling.

"Sure and they're in heaven praying for us now," he said. And if any of us criticized any of the Koreans in his presence: "Now, now, remember his mother loves him. He's just misguided, the poor lad."

The Yalu River was less than a mile away, but the guards would not allow water to be fetched more than once a day. I was told there were G.I.'s—I could not check this personally—who did not have water for five days and who died of thirst.

The water was brought in fifty-gallon drums on a cart pulled by G.I.'s. The pull was over a bumpy road, and the men on duty were thoroughly splashed. The water froze immediately, and the G.I.'s pulling the cart returned looking like weird creatures from Scandinavian folklore. Frequently, frostbite followed, and infection, then death.

A room was set aside for the sick. The frostbitten were put into it. There was no fire in the room and the floor was bare. The door was nailed shut, and the patients were left alone. No one went near the room for two days. When the door was opened, all the occupants were dead.

The kitchen was hell. A crew of American cooks tried to prepare food. They were supervised by guards who kicked, screamed, insulted, made the cooks change the food from pot to pot, made them put out the fires, then light them again. As a result, only one meal a day was prepared, and it was usually ready around midnight. The distribution, because of the blackout, took place in the dark, and many were left without food.

The corridors were filthy, because the G.I.'s with dysentery could not get to the lavatories quickly enough. And every morning, bodies were taken out and put under the straw in the courtyard. Internees were dying of dysentery, pneumonia, and thirst.

Walter Eltringham, the ECA engineer, saw I had some water in a bottle.

"I'm dying," he said. "I mean it. I haven't had a drink in two days. Give me a gulp."

That night, because there had been a raid on the nearby town, Chung Kang Djin, we were moved to a neighboring village called Ha Djang Nee. The population was turned out, and their houses and the school were given over to us. On the way there Walter Eltringham collapsed. He died, without recovering consciousnes, the next day.

The "special group" of diplomats and journalists was kept waiting outside a house for three hours in the extreme cold while the other prisoners were being billeted. Then we were told to walk into the house before which we had stood all this time. The house had belonged to a tobacconist, whose chests took up a lot of space. The diplomats and journalists, together with the seven Koreans, had a room twelve feet by twelve—for seventeen people. Captain Vyvyan Holt and Norman Owen collapsed with pneumonia as soon as we entered the house. Soon they were delirious with fever. Amelia Martel, the seventy-six-year-old mother of one the French diplomats, went down with a violent attack of beri-beri. Her limbs became swollen and the skin burst. Her heart was fast weakening. The authorities decided to move us then, and we were taken to another house.

During our stay at Ha Djang Nee from November 17, 1950, to February 2, 1951, we changed quarters three times. The average accommodation was seven people to a room nine feet by nine feet. The worst was during the month of January—ten to a room nine feet by nine. We stayed packed like that for a whole month. The wood supply was not sufficient to provide heating. One of the officers told us that faggots had to be brought twenty miles, that there was no fuel any nearer in this denuded country. Food consisted of a quantity of grain a day—we were told it was six hundred grams—and one stringy Chinese cabbage a day for about ten persons. There were some distributions of oil in very small quantities. Meat was issued in small quantities on a number of occasions. Sugar and white rice were given to the sick, but the issues were unpredictable. On January 1, 1951, there was a large meal of pork, rice, vegetables, and peanuts.

The diplomats and journalists were given canvas sacks filled with straw to use as mattresses. They had been given thin padded cotton clothes on December 15; the other internees did not receive warm clothing until the second week in January.

A barber was brought from Chung Kang Djin for the special group; he told us that the thermometer outside the lumber-company office showed forty degrees below zero. And still we had no winter footwear. In sandals or rags, we had to attend food distributions, waiting sometimes three to four hours for our rations. When we returned to our billets, our co-inmates would crowd around us to help us warm up. It took a very long time.

The food distribution took place in the courtyard of a house used as a hospital. Waiting there to get our grain and cabbage, we watched emaciated youngsters, without trousers, move their bones slowly over the frozen ground to get to the side of the house. Some of them could not wait till they left the courtyard, and we watched helplessly while the guards kicked the offending prisoners, prisoners at the point of death.

Occasionally, one of the Korean quartermasters would drop a cabbage leaf. On all fours, snarling like dogs, we would fight over it. Diplomats, missionaries, soldiers, journalists, we fought for a cabbage leaf.

Once a guard dropped a cigarette butt. Two of the dying youngsters, moving with horrifying slowness, got down to the ground and crawled like insects towards the smoking butt. They reached their objective together. Slowly, they raised their arms, and slowly, they hit each other. You could hear bone hit bone, and you could see the brittle skin

121

part, uncovering the bone. They gasped and moaned as they fought. When one of them fell to the ground, the other moved to pick up the spoils. The cigarette butt had burned out.

Later that day, in the field behind our house, I met a tall man who was trying to get up after squatting down because of dysentery. I helped him. He asked me who I was. I told him.

"I am Thompson," he said, "of the *Valley Forge*. You do not recognize me, do you? You've changed a lot yourself. I'm dying." He was the Corsair pilot whom I had met six months before, his body bruised with beatings, at the Communist Army headquarters near Suwon. I could not have identified him now.

"Nonsense," I told him. "You'll pull through. You mustn't give up."

"I'm not giving up. I don't want to die. I'm fighting to stay alive, but I can't do it. There's not enough food, and the boys looking after us in this hospital are eating most of it anyhow. I don't blame them. We can't be saved without drugs now. One case of medicine would bring us life. I want you to tell my mother. You must not let yourself die. Let them know back home. A case of pills would save us. Trucks come all the time. My God! We called them our allies. When we marched through Manpo, there was a Russian big shot in a limousine grinning as we passed. You've got to get out, Deane, and tell the story."

I felt that Thompson, U.S.N., had given me a commission. I watched for him. The next day, his tall skin-covered

skeleton, thrown over a pole, was carried away towards the
burial ground. I tried to follow his burial party, to say
good-by. One of the guards kicked me away. I stood outside our house and watched till I could see no more. I
tried to recite what I remembered of the naval burial
service. Then someone called me for water-carrying
duty.

We had to carry the water from a well two hundred
yards away. The well rope was frozen solid and stuck to
our hands. The bucket leaked so much that we always
brought it up half empty. In that way we filled a twenty-
five gallon drum which had to be carried between two of
us, slung on a pole.

"I always hated water," said M. Perruche, the French
chargé d'affaires from Seoul, nursing his fingers burned by
the frozen rope and somehow managing to smile, "but
after this I'll even wash my teeth with wine."

At the well, information was exchanged, and it was the
only place where we of the special group could come into
contact with the American P.O.W.'s. There the water-
carrying skeletons told us what news they had.

Some new prisoners had arrived in December, 1950.
They had been caught near a big reservoir in northeastern
Korea by Chinese troops, whom they were surprised to
see. They were inspected by a Chinese officer, who gave
them cigarettes and a good meal of chicken, and told them
they could rejoin their own forces. Then they were left to
their own devices, and set off on foot in what they thought
was the right direction. They passed Chinese soldiers, who

123

did not seem at all interested in these G.I.'s. That night, exhausted by the marching and the cold, they lay down to sleep, and when they awoke their feet were so frostbitten that they could not stand up. They lay for two days in a little wood, and then some Chinese troops came upon them. They were moved to a field hospital, where their wounds were treated with penicillin; then they were taken across into Manchuria in mule carts. In a People's Hospital, a Chinese surgeon operated on them, amputating some of their toes. They were told by the Chinese that the war would soon be over, that it was sure to be over by Christmas; and after arriving at our camp they expressed the opinion that this was probably correct, because they had heard, before they were captured, of MacArthur's speech to the troops, in which he promised they would be "home for Christmas." Thus grew the legend of negotiations going on, of a *de facto* truce on some line. That was December, 1950, and we could no longer hear the explosions we had heard in November—those explosions that had raised such hopes.

"I tell you, sir, I've been with the artillery now for twelve years. I can tell a 105 when it's booming. Those are our 105's, you can take it from me."

"How far do you think they are from here?"

"Of course it's difficult to tell over mountainous territory, but I should guess not more than twenty miles."

What news for the others at the hut! And he had said he guessed these wonderful guns were only twenty miles away! They might be farther away, and yet they might be nearer.

And the next day there was another version.

"I tell you, sir, I've been with the mortars now for ten years. If that noise doesn't come from our three-inchers then I'll eat my hat, dirty and lousy as it is."

The noises sounded pretty much like those of the day before, but perhaps that was just faulty hearing. That American officer was an expert. We hurried back to tell the others in the hut.

One day there was a speech by the second-in-command of the camp, a tall, dry Korean captain who seemed to have much authority and was apparently the political officer of the staff.

"There is an old proverb," he told us diplomats and journalists, "which says that the Chinese and the Koreans are like the lips and the teeth—very close. We help each other. You cannot eat well if you have only lips or only teeth. You must have both. Together we are chasing the Americans. They are running away like drowned rats, embarking in our ports, which they soiled with their presence, and leaving behind them enormous quantities of materiel, thousands of cars, guns, jeeps. Together with the Chinese, we are chasing them into the water with our bayonets, giving them no respite. The war will soon be over. We shall liberate our country, throw out the foreign invaders, and you will soon go home."

The Tiger made a speech, too.

"We are winning great victories. We are destroying big U.N. forces. It is not true what MacArthur said—it was not four hundred of your planes that we burned on the ground at Kimpo, but one thousand. We are winning. We, the Koreans, are the greatest fighters in the world. We have defeated fifty-three nations. One Korean soldier is better than ten Americans. We do not need weapons to fight you and to win. We shall be victorious very soon and you will go home to your families."

"When? Before Christmas?"

"No, not before Christmas, but everything will be all right by the end of February. I am telling you officially."

The fellow seemed so certain. Yet all this talk about chasing drowning rats, burning planes, making us run before them, could not be true. Surely it was Korean boasting, a face-saving device of the Communist Government to explain its acceptance of U.N. truce proposals. After all, the United Nations Command, with the Pyongyang plain in its hands, had very strong bargaining power. After all, the purpose of the war was to save South Korea from the Communists. When our troops crossed the Parallel, we told ourselves, surely they did so only because the Communists would not accept negotiation, because they had to be forced into negotiation. The Reds had finally seen the light, and all this talk of victories was just their way of telling their people they had lost. The war had surely stopped, and the U.N. troops had evacuated some parts of North

Korea. All we were waiting for was the Red Cross. In a ravaged country it was difficult to move prisoners. It would probably take some time. That was why the Tiger was so sure that "everything would be all right by the end of February." He had already been given a date, probably. And if the war was not finished, then why did our planes not bomb the international bridge at Chung Kang Djin, over which, as we could see, a ceaseless stream of trucks passed? Why did they not fly over any more? That last was our strongest argument.

So we reasoned, reveling in hope—the only thing that was left to us. We built arguments on nothing, illogically, childishly perhaps, but we had to do it, to keep alive the hope on which we fed.

On January 4, 1951, some of our guards went to a march-past in Chung Kang Djin to celebrate the "second liberation" of Seoul from the "Anglo-American imperialists." Some of the Chinese who visited us gave information. A farmer who had listened to a U.N. broadcast in Korean contributed some more. Slowly, reluctantly, we built up a picture of the situation which we knew to be true. Seoul had been captured again. The United Nations had retreated, abandoning all its "negotiation trumps," and abandoning us. They were still retreating, and thousands of Chinese, in brand new Molotov trucks, were pouring south in a new effort to capture Pusan. We fought against this picture, not wanting to take it in, trying hard to believe it could not be true, until one night, as if by previous arrangement, we admitted the truth to ourselves and drowned our despair in song through half the night.

Mr. Moon, who lived next door to us, was intrigued by this burst of choral optimism.

"Mr. Deane," he said to me the next morning in the courtyard, "you have good news, no?"

"No."

"Why you sing last night?"

"We just felt like singing."

"You sing very happy songs, no?"

"Yes."

"So you are very happy, no?"

"No."

"Mr. Deane, when I have good news, I tell you. Why you not tell me?"

"I have no good news, only bad."

Mr. Moon was offended. He went away and contemplated the sun. Perhaps he was more offended than usual, for he was going through a difficult period. He had been deposed from leadership. Mr. Chang had discovered a cousin among the Korean officers of the Tiger's staff, and through him he had told the authorities that Moon Hak Pong really desired the defeat of the North and was intriguing with the diplomats. The statements of Mr. Chang were corroborated by Mr. Chaigh, and Mr. Moon was removed from the special-group billet to a "cold room" used for punishing recalcitrant internees. We could see the

128

Tiger visiting that room every day, just as he had done when Commissioner Lord had been given the cold-room treatment.

That had been some time before. Commissioner Lord was taken away from his hut and marched off to the cold room. He told me about it later. The next morning he was visited by the Tiger, who was twirling his pistol round his trigger finger.

"Are you ready to confess?" asked the Tiger.

"Confess what?" said the Commissioner.

The Tiger took aim at the Commissioner's head.

"Don't be insolent. You know I can shoot you. Are you going to confess?"

"Well, sir, if you give me some indication as to what you want me to say, I shall say it."

"Perhaps I had better shoot you," said the Tiger, releasing the safety catch, "or perhaps I'll give you till tomorrow."

That performance, with variations, was repeated every morning for a fortnight. One evening another officer came in to see the Commissioner.

"Ah," he said, "you no longer wear your insignia on your tunic. Why?"

"The commanding officer of the camp made me take them off."

"He was jealous, because your uniform looked better. Empty your pockets."

129

The Commissioner placed on the floor before him a key ring, a pair of nail clippers, a ball-point pen, and a wallet.

The Korean picked up the pen and the wallet.

"Do you need these?"

"No. I would like you to have them."

The Korean put the pen in his pocket, pulled out a small mirror, and admired the effect of the pen-clip on his uniform.

"Oh no," he said, "I could not take it really." He filled the wallet with some North Korean banknotes.

"This is a nice wallet. Do you want it?"

"I'd be honored if you took it."

"I couldn't really," said the Korean, putting it in his pocket and rising. "Look, when the major comes to see you, be careful what you say. Do not make him angry. If you make him angry he will shoot you. You know he shoots easily. So do as he says; otherwise he becomes very angry. Don't contradict him, and I shall see if I can help you. I really cannot take your pen and your wallet," and he walked out.

The next day, the Commissioner was taken to the Tiger's office and made to kneel.

"Well," said the Tiger, "will you confess now?"

"Sir, I will confess, if you tell me what you want."

"You don't know?"

"No, sir."

"You lie. You know very well that in the group to which I appointed you as a leader there has been trouble. The

White Russians have been quarreling with the Tartars, and both of them with the missionaries. You never reported that trouble to me, and that was your duty. Do you confess now?"

"Yes, sir. I am sorry."

"Why did you not report?"

"I did not want to worry you, knowing what important questions occupied your mind."

"It is my business to know everything."

"I realize it now, and I confess."

"Your organization, the Salvation Army, what is it exactly? Write down all the details about the organization, and especially about the work in Korea."

Commissioner Lord wrote for two hours. The Tiger took the paper. He did not look at it.

"You have been doing charitable work in Korea. We Koreans do not need your interference. If I catch you doing the work of your organization again I will shoot you. Now you may go back to your companions," and the Tiger tore the Commissioner's report into small pieces without having even looked at it.

Mr. Moon did not stay as long as the Commissioner in the cold room. He returned to us in four days. Mr. Chaigh was immediately put under arrest and taken away.

"Mr. Chang also very bad man," Mr. Moon told me, "but he has strong friend. I wait. I remember."

While Mr. Chaigh was away, we lived under the reign

of Mr. Chang. He did not rule personally. He had Big Mr. Pak appointed as leader of the special group, and he ruled Big Mr. Pak with a rod of iron.

Daily, the North Korean officer who was Mr. Chang's cousin would come to our courtyard and confer there with his relative, making insulting remarks aloud about Mr. Moon, whose presence he demanded. The other Korean internees gathered around and gloated. Mr. Moon was martyred but very dignified. Later in the day, patiently, he would start working on one, then on the other of his compatriots. He knew a lot about their past careers which they wanted to keep from the Communists, and Mr. Moon used the power his knowledge gave him. Soon he had them all denouncing one another to the Communists. Mr. Chaigh was doing his bit during his interviews with the Tiger in the cold room. As the price of his return to our billet he wrote in Chinese characters what our French sinologists described as an exquisite hymn to the Korean People's Army. When he came back, he threw himself headlong into political intrigues, although very weakened by his five days without any heating. As a result the camp administration did not know who among the detained South Korean politicians was most reliable—or, at best, the least sincere. So it was decided to hold an examination in dialectical materialism, and the Short Course in the History of the Communist Party of the Soviet Union. Some of us—it must be said—coached Mr. Moon.

It was an oral examination, with the political officer in

the chair, and the seven candidates squatting on the floor around him. After the examiner left, Mr. Moon came out, looking impassive.

"I am leader now," he said and went off for some sun contemplation.

Mr. Moon took over leadership with a firm hand. He was still being insulted daily by Mr. Chang's cousin, the North Korean officer, but Mr. Moon could be patient. He changed the cooking arrangements. The wife of the farmer in whose house we were quartered was to do the cooking for us, and she was going to get part of our fuel ration, as well as all our food. Mr. Moon started eating with the farmer—special little dishes, extra tidbits. He stopped losing weight. Our rations went down. We rebelled. Mr. Moon called a council at which he defended his policy. Outside, the farmer paced up and down, listening in, very anxious to know the result of our confabulations. A compromise was reached—the farmer's wife was to continue cooking, but we were to measure the supplies she was given. The farmer did not like that. Mr. Moon gave him some tobacco, which he seemed to produce from nowhere, talked to him about these "foreign devils" and continued eating his extra tidbits. He managed to sell one of the diplomat's watches and a lighter, in exchange for some food to save the invalids, and he revealed himself a first-class cook, producing for the sick some delicious glutinous dishes out of practically nothing. True, he ate half of what he cooked, but then that was Mr. Moon.

133

Mr. Moon ate the food of the sick without bothering to hide his actions, as his colleagues did, for Mr. Moon was not ashamed of his actions. And he did try to be kind, even to the old grandmother who lived in the farmhouse and whom everybody treated contemptuously. The children ragged her, her daughter screamed at her, her son-in-law made her work like a beast of burden, and she did not have enough clothes to cover her body. Mr. Moon treated her courteously, and the old woman idolized the politician, going to the extent of stealing from her son-in-law's storehouse to feed Mr. Moon.

One other person was nice to the grandmother, and that was the farmer's little eleven-year-old girl, who had just crossed the great divide between childhood and responsibility. Little girls in Korea, up to the age of ten, are not disciplined in any way. They have all privileges and no responsibilities. They do as they like. They scream, have tantrums, are insolent and insubordinate, and no one attempts to correct them. Within the limitations of extreme poverty, they are granted whatever they wish. They are waited upon hand and foot; they have enough to eat even if that means starving the grandmother to death. Then comes the tenth birthday.

A baby brother or sister—there is always one—is put on the back of yesterday's child, who today is grown-up because she is ten. A five-gallon tin is placed on her head, and she carries water all day from the distant well. With a short-handled digging instrument in her hand and baby

134

brother on her back, she works for long hours in the fields. She lights the fire, carries wood, and takes second place or worse at the food distribution. The stubborn spoiled child with the flashing satisfied smile acquires—from one day to the next—the lines of care and worry, and in the eleven-year-old face one already sees the neglected grandmother.

That little eleven-year-old farm girl, in all her suffering, despite her backbreaking toil, found time to notice me and to commiserate. Furtively, from time to time, she slipped me a turnip, some scrapings from her mother's pot, a head of garlic. And when I tried to get out in the sun, she would come, squat near me, and smile. With bits of different-colored sorghum stalks and with some thread pulled out of my rags I made her a gaudy necklace—yellow, red, and black beads alternating. She took it shyly, hung it around her neck, bent her head, trying to see how it looked. With her frostbitten hand, she patted it clumsily, gave me a smile, blushed furiously, and ran away, losing one of the torn rubber slippers she wore.

I picked up the abandoned footwear of this little Asiatic Cinderella and carried it to her house. I found her crying. The necklace was no longer around her neck. Mama had given it to baby brother, aged two, who was busily tearing it to pieces. I wanted to pat her head and tell her I would make her another, but one does not do that to little girls over ten in North Korea, and they do not expect it, for nature is cruel, and they have come to recognize this fact.

In Korea, cocks are allowed to fight till they kill one another, and to egg them on to greater excitement red pepper is rubbed into their eyes. Newly born calves are allowed to spend the night in the open at 70 degrees below freezing. Many die. The puppy which grows as the children's pet is put in a sack and beaten to death slowly so that the meat will be tenderer for eating. Death and pain are such commonplace things in the mountains of North Korea, they do not shock the inhabitants of that rugged country. That is why, perhaps, with the cold at its highest, their miserable hovel burned out by some strange machine for reasons they do not understand, they sit outside in the road and hardly moan. What has happened to them is not really remarkable. It is just another installment of pain and death. These things have to be, and in the summer there will be more puppies, more calves, more babies, and it will be possible to dig the now frozen earth to get clay for the new mud hut. It's hard to defeat them, because they are already defeated, they have nothing to lose.

CHAPTER 6

Indoctrination

MR. MOON loathed us. We backed him occasionally because we thought him amusing. Although the diplomats tried to hide this, Mr. Moon knew, and his dignity could not stand it; but he always hoped for a possible comeback of the West, and people like us, to his way of thinking, could be useful. Still, he did not like facetiousness.

On New Year's Day, 1951, we had a surprise. Instead of the usual millet and cabbage leaf, we were given a small pig for the seventeen of us (ten Europeans, seven Koreans), rice, oil, turnips, some potatoes, onions, garlic, red pepper, and peanuts. Mr. Moon took charge of the cooking, turned everyone out of the kitchen, blocked all the holes through which he knew we watched, and after five hours produced a succulent meal. There was far less meat than we had expected, and Mr. Moon did not seem to have much of an appetite left. Still, we thanked him, and when we had all finished, gesturing broadly, he made a speech, in English, not using one of us as interpreter—this to annoy Mr. Chang, who spoke only Korean.

"Today we begin New Year. Today we begin New Life. Today we all stop troubles"—there had been much sedition in his flock—"today we all good friends, no?"

"No!" whispered Owen, unable to resist the tempting question.

Mr. Moon heard him. He pursed his eyes and kept silent for a while.

"Today we start new life. All friends now and help one another make much difficulties little."

He was interrupted by the exaggerated snorting of Mr. Chang. We tiptoed out, and for hours, in the room of the seven South Korean politicians, fiery but elaborate insults were flung across the room. Altogether it was not a bad New Year's Day. It would have been better if our stomachs had not rebelled against the rich food. It all went to waste. Mr. Moon did not speak to us for several days. He thought it was our example that had set off insubordination in the group, and he was not a man to take such things lightly. Still angry, he complained about us to a new guard who was impressed by the politician's command of honorifics.

This guard kicked open our door, pointed his rifle at each of us in turn, took a deep breath and said very quickly in Japanese:

"If you look down on Korean people you will be shot if you despise General Kim Il Sung you will be shot if you think bad thoughts about the Republic you will be shot if you conspire against the camp authorities you will be shot." As an afterthought he added: "You must wash your hands and face three times a day and your feet once a day."

The wells had run dry. Water was rationed. We had not been able to wash for many weeks.

The guard lowered his rifle and squatted. He asked for tobacco and, as we had none, he pulled some out of his pocket and rolled himself a cigarette.

"This war would be over by now," he said, "if it were not for these terrible Hawaiians who will go on fighting. They are over seven feet tall, and they fight and fight. You are very queer people. Why do you have big noses? You like big noses, do you not? The girls in Seoul gave themselves injections in the nose to make it big so that you would like them. Why do you want our women? We do not take yours."

Then he ordered us to have a general clean-up. It was the third that day. Whenever a guard wanted he could make us turn out our room, take the straw sacks off the floor, sweep the mud walls, and leave the door open for aeration. That was to fight disease, they said.

Our doors were made of thin paper. Keeping the room warm was hard. These frequent aerations made the rooms icy. And we had to carry out the sick, laying them on the ground at seventy degrees below freezing. When we protested once, on the grounds that we had already cleaned the room twice that day, the North Korean officer who was the cousin of Mr. Chang called us dirty pigs and screamed. We had to obey. Two of us made a remark to each other.

Mr. Chang's cousin separated us immediately and asked us what it was we had said. Luckily it was innocuous, and luckily we both had the sense to tell the truth, otherwise, if our stories had not tallied, we would have landed in the "cold room."

Besides turning out the rooms, to "preserve our health," the authorities wet our clothes with carbolic solution, and made us do calisthenics at dawn. One of the officers had another method for preserving health. He came into our hut and saw me lying on the floor.

"Why is that man ill? I order him to be well. If you are not well tomorrow, I will send you to the cold room."

Next time he came, I pretended I was well.

Chinese officials from across the river frequently came to watch us while we were being disinfected or bullied into "health." They stood in a group, their hands tucked in the sleeves of their well-padded dark blue suits, grinning embarrassedly. Meadmore, our Chinese expert, talked to them, and gleaned information. As soon as they realized he was using them, they would retreat a few steps and go on looking.

At other times they'd come while we fed. The guard would fling open the door and stand by while the august guests viewed the feeding beasts. Although our dignity demanded that we should stop eating, our hunger won the day. We hated these visitors more perhaps even than those guards who had hit us.

"When I visit the zoo," said someone, "I always take

peanuts for the monkeys. They give us nothing, not even a cigarette."

And they had plenty of cigarettes.

Soon after our arrival in Ha Djang Nee, indoctrination and "education" were started. The Koreans said they were very anxious that the prisoners should not let themselves brood, that they should be happy, that they should organize themselves like the guards.

"Look," said the indoctrinator, "I've put a blackboard here. Now you must rid yourselves of the survivals of capitalism and become our brothers. We believe in criticism and self-criticism. I will start this self-criticism by telling you I have not always done all I could for you. I am sorry. I will do more in the future. And now criticism. The guard who is on duty now has behaved badly: we shall punish him. Haven't any of you something to say? Please, won't someone confess? All right, perhaps you do not want to do it openly. Write it on the blackboard, when I am gone."

Later that day he came back and looked at the blank blackboard. Then he brought out his flute and started playing for the benefit of the G.I.'s in the freezing schoolroom.

"Please," said the indoctrinator, "won't those of you who are well let the sick come near the stove?"

Nobody moved. The sick were kept away from the stove by those who were well. Captivity and ill-treatment breed selfishness as well as self-sacrifice.

Lessons in American history were given. The annihilation of the Red Indians by the settlers was stressed. Colored and Filipino boys were challenged about racial discrimination, about "Jim Crow" segregation and lynching. Instances of brutality towards the colored people were stressed. Mark Twain's caustic comments on American Army behavior in the Philippines had obviously been incorporated in the indoctrinator's notebook. Charles Dickens was quoted as an authority on living conditions in Britain. The conditions described by Dickens, according to the indoctrinator, still prevailed, "altered somewhat in form but not in essence."

"You came to attack us," he told the Americans. "We never attacked America. It was your President Theodore Roosevelt who made possible the Japanese conquest of our country. Before that, one of your admirals bombarded our country to make us trade with the West. We did not want to have anything to do with you and yet you forced yourselves upon us. And now you come again. In spite of it all we do not hate you. We want to treat you well, if you will let us. You are having a bad time, but so are we. The whole country is ruined by your planes. There is nothing left. We give you all we can."

He tried to show the G.I.'s that before the Korean war the Communists were rebuilding North Korea while the Americans were exploiting the South. "Some of you are peasants. You know what it means to have your own land. We gave land to the farmers who before had worked for

142

others. We made all our factories work and built new ones. Some of you were in Seoul before this war started. You saw the coolies waiting for jobs, the factories that were closed. Perhaps some of you have known unemployment. You know what it feels like. Some of you remember the Depression. Tell the others after I have gone what it was like."

Before this war we did not have your skyscrapers, your automobiles, but we did not have unemployed, either. Anyone who wanted to work honestly could do so, and support himself. Some did not go hungry while others had too much. Everyone had an equal chance, and we were building fast, much faster relatively than in your countries, where vested interests bury important inventions to keep their profits high, to keep on exploiting you, and to make you pay many times more than you need for the daily necessities of life."

The indoctrinator came to visit the special group of journalists and diplomats to announce that on the next day he would begin teaching us "Marxism-Leninism." This was a preliminary breaking of the ground. He was very pleasant, and offered cigarettes—the first we had seen for three months, though we had been given some tobacco. Perruche and Meadmore, together with Captain Holt—who, weakened by illness, was only just able to speak—capped all the indoctrinator's quotations.

"Lenin," said the indoctrinator, "wrote in *Left Communism, an Infantile Disorder,* that . . ."

143

"Aha!" answered Captain Holt, "but you must not forget that Stalin, in his interview with the first American workers who visited the Soviet Union in 1926, said . . ."

"And"—this from Meadmore—"Marx, in *Misère de la Philosophie, Réponse à la Philosophie de la Misère de M. Proudhon,* states . . ."

After half an hour of this the baby-faced indoctrinator left. He never returned to begin the lessons he had promised us. Instead, he continued with the G.I.'s. But the odds were against him. Everyone was very cold. The school in which most of the G.I.'s were housed was heated by a barrel stove, which smoked so much that it was a case of choosing between suffocation and freezing. There was not enough food. Dr. Ernst Kisch calculated its calorific value at approximately 700 (approximately 1500 calories are generally accepted as the minimum subsistence level). The type of food, according to Dr. Kisch, was directly harmful to those suffering from dysentery—which meant almost all of us.

Yet some were converted, some who later, without pressure—this is third-hand information but from reliable sources—joined the so-called Red Star Club, the Peace Committee of the American and British P.O.W.'s in North Korea. Why were they convinced? The answer lies in their background, in their education, and it is an individual answer for each one of the converts to the Communist faith. If one must generalize, these converts were impressed by the way the Communist case was presented.

The non-Communist case had never been put as impressively to these converts—if it had been put at all.

But this applies to real Red converts, not to those who joined the Red Star Club to get more food. I cannot blame these men. Their ideological ruse perhaps saved them from death, and from the "hospitals."

There were "hospitals" in the camp, houses that had been set apart, and to which the dying were carried. There was so little space that none could lie flat: they died in a sitting position. They died of pneumonia, of meningitis, of dysentery—sometimes of all three together. They were cared for by a man who claimed he was a second-year medical student of Pyongyang University. This man would not allow the two qualified doctors interned in the camp to diagnose or treat the patients. The United States Army doctor was made to carry the Korean medical student's tray of instruments, but was not allowed to enter the patients' rooms.

Captain Holt and Norman Owen, the British pro-consul, had fallen seriously ill with pneumonia and dysentery. Their temperatures rose to 106.7 degrees. The Tiger was alarmed. The medical student left on a five-day trek to bring back three penicillin injections for Captain Holt and twelve sulfapyridine tablets for Owen. This helped, but the temperatures did not drop. Then they both had a relapse. Somewhere in the fields near the house we had found a broken metal vessel which we used as a chamber pot. According to Dr. Kisch, one of the reasons the G.I.'s were dying so rapidly was that, while suffering from pneumonia, they had to go out to the toilet in their summer clothes in seventy degrees below freezing. The house of the "special group" had the immense privilege of owning a broken vessel. Perhaps that is why Holt and Owen lived.

While nursing them, I slept between Holt and Owen in our hut. One morning as I sat, I noticed a stream of lice crawling away from their bodies and towards me, and suddenly I remembered the story that vermin leave a dying man. I felt very frightened. A few more lice did not matter —I already had thousands—but the story terrified me. The North Korean medical student came in just then and discovered that the temperature of both the patients was over 106°F.

They were completely delirious. Owen was certain there were ambulances outside ready to take him home, and he fought me time and again to get out of the room. At other times both the sick imagined there were stacks of chicken sandwiches in the room. They accused me of stealing their share. They complained of hunger, but could not keep down the rough boiled rice which was the only thing we could give them.

The North Korean medical student ordered them to be carried to one of the "hospitals." M. Martel, chancellor of the French Legation in Seoul, fought for the two men. Faced by a maddened, screaming young man who was not accustomed to "insubordination" from internees, Martel, imperturbable as ever, produced elaborate arguments

146

in honorific Japanese, and won the day. The British Minister and his pro-consul were not removed to the "hospital" where they would have sat, unable to stretch, until they died.

Bishop Patrick Burns, the Apostolic Delegate, whose diplomatic status the Koreans had persistently refused to recognize, died in one of the "hospitals." He was fetched late at night. He was boiling with fever and fading fast. His companions begged that the Bishop be allowed to die where he was. The guards were adamant. The dying prelate was dragged to one of the "hospitals" and made to squat among the other dying inmates. Monsignor Thomas Quinlan had somehow obtained permission to visit his friend. Bishop Burns managed a smile.

"Tom," he whispered, "don't be sad. I have always wanted to lay down my life for our faith and the Good Lord has given me this privilege. Look after yourself and the others."

The next morning the Monsignor went to see the Bishop. He found him dead, his hands clasped as if in prayer, a smile on his face. Thomas Quinlan stripped off his soutane with the red piping, dressed the dead Bishop in it and carried him to his grave. The guards did not like long funerals, but their threats could not move the tall, Irish priest who, bareheaded in the fearsome cold, recited by heart the burial service.

Had they let him, the Monsignor would have gladly rendered this service to all the dead. But funerals were

147

summary affairs. Six times a day, sometimes seven, G.I.'s would pass with a corpse bent double over a pole. The carriers often slipped and fell. Once, one of the carriers never got up again. He had died on his way to bury the dead.

Father Canavan died, a citizen of Eire—a country which did not even belong to the United Nations. When he was being dragged to the "hospital" he voiced for the last time, in his inimitable brogue, the jocular phrase that had become his trade mark:

"If you think this is bad, you should have seen what the British did to the Irish."

Matti, a Swiss, another neutral, died from pneumonia and dysentery. An old White Russian, with no nationality, also died, exhausted by the ordeal he had undergone. More and more died. To keep Holt and Owen alive, we begged for extra food, and when refused we stole it. They lived, but they were the exceptions. Almost no one recovered from pneumonia.

Some caught pneumonia because they were made to kneel in the snow. From our house we could see G.I.'s on their knees outside their billets. The guard, walking up and down, frequently kicked the kneeling men. We wondered why this was done. We were soon to find out for ourselves that it could be done on the flimsiest pretext. On December 5, 1950, an interned South Korean politician asked George Blake and me, who were on water-carrying duty, to fetch four twenty-five gallon drums of water instead of three, because, he said, he wanted to do some laundry. We answered that we were too exhausted. The South Korean politician complained to the guard, saying that we "looked down on the Korean people." The guard ordered George Blake and myself to kneel down in the snow. He accused us of insulting the Koreans, and of not carrying the amount of water laid down in regulations. We replied that this was not so. The guard said he would teach us not to lie, and he beat us with the butt of his rifle, kicked us and slapped us. George, who got the worst of it, smiled throughout the ordeal, his left eyebrow cocked ironically at the guard, his Elizabethan beard aggressively thrust forward. The guard walked away, and some time later—I do not know how much later—he came and told us that if we admitted we had lied he would let us go. The temperature was forty degrees below. We admitted we had lied. The following day the Tiger said we should not have lied, and indicated that the guard had been punished for hitting us. When next he was on duty that guard tried to apologize.

But disease and privations were not the only killers. There were G.I.'s who would give up a day's food for one cigarette rolled in old newspaper, and—I am sorry, it is true—there were G.I.'s who bought food at the price of another man's life. There were those who worked in the cookhouse and stole their comrades' food. There were those who stripped their skeletic, dying companions, hours before they died. But, by and large, those were the exceptions. There were those who not only succeeded in preserving their human dignity but tried to explain—to me, a journalist—the others who had failed.

Among those who could take it, the most remarkable—or rather one of the most remarkable, for there were many—was a ginger-headed teen-ager called Jesse Sizemore. Jesse got pneumonia, then dysentery, and I saw him when he'd been worn down to a shadow, barely able to crawl from his hut to the field. Once, when I helped him, he smiled, winked, and said:

"Watch me recover, Deane. I'm aiming to go back to my pa's farm. I ain't going to die here."

He made a remarkably fast recovery and volunteered for duty in the "dysentery hospital" where no one wanted to work. He did not eat his wards' food. Still weak himself, he worked tirelessly to save others, and somehow, he kept always cheerful. Even the most unpleasant guards liked him.

"Letting a G.I. die in my hospital is something I won't do," he told me. They still died in his "hospital," though less quickly than in others. But the death rate kept climbing.

Across the river, not half a mile away, in China, a ceaseless procession of brand new Molotov trucks kept passing. One of them could have brought a case of drugs to our camp and saved the lives of many. One of those trucks did bring a case for our camp once. It contained propaganda literature—magazines plastered with pictures of

Mrs. Monica Felton and the Dean of Canterbury, with captions praising the system that was letting these American youngsters die.

And these young Americans went on dying. There had been 777 when we joined them in September, 1950, and more than sixty percent of them had died by February 2, 1951, when an elderly Korean major took our special group of diplomats and journalists away.

CHAPTER 7

Fatso's "Camp"

"POLITICAL conditions have changed," the elderly major told us. "You are being taken elsewhere." More he would not say.

The major was accompanied by a North Korean police sergeant with a tommygun, who made us line up and then march to a bus that seemed to be serving a regular route for the use of the civilian population. It was a ramshackle old Japanese vehicle run on charcoal, with no windows, and a wooden bench down each side. It was packed so full that we thought it was bound to break its chassis, yet at every stop more and more people came in. Everyone had someone else on his lap, and there was no question of getting out for a short walk. Only the driver could do that. One member of our party, wedged in a corner by four elderly Korean women who seemed to have gone irretrievably to sleep, wet his pants when the extreme cold and the long wait made control impossible. At one stop a common criminal prisoner was brought in, his arms tied behind his back. His mother and father were weeping beside the bus, watched by the prisoner's escort. Before taking leave of their son, they gave his guard a wad of money and a bottle of rice spirits.

We spent the night in a town we had passed during the death march. It had been quite large, with a number of public buildings, a hospital, and some schools. There were only three huts left. One of these was a "People's Kitchen."

At last in a warm room, we watched our elderly major ordering food. Young teen-age girls brought a table, then bowls of resplendent white rice and soybean-curd soup. There was pepper on the table and soy sauce. We could not believe our eyes. Having wolfed down our meal we asked for more, and there was more. Then we slept, waking to board the bus again. Our seats had been taken, but our armed police sergeant made their occupants get up for us to sit.

We left the bus a few miles from Manpo, at the town near which Lt. Cordus H. Thornton had been murdered. The bus was going south and we were going north. Would we mind a short walk to the frontier town?

We walked with the major, whom we had nicknamed "Uncle," and he talked: We were going to be billeted in a private house with much more room than we'd had before. Did we like goat meat? And honey? Could we drink milk? And this white bread the police sergeant had—was it to our liking? Books? Oh, there would be plenty of books. What kind would we like? Classics? The libraries were sure to have them. And how about music? Did we

153

like Far Eastern music or would we prefer Western music? He would get us a player and records. Perhaps we would like a radio set. That would be easy to arrange. Of course, there would be electric light and a bathroom. Our life would get better and better every day. We reached Manpo, a little later than Madame Martel, whom Uncle had put on a bullock cart. In the middle of the town stood a large concrete railway bridge, intact.

Around the bridge, nearly every building was blasted or burnt to the ground. Here and there a scrap of ruin stood up incongruously amid the reeking wreckage—the strong-room of a bank, the cement pillars supporting a crumpled metal boiler, the concrete chimney of a school. The bridge —the choice target—was untouched.

The few remaining buildings were occupied by the police and their families. In one of them we met the young major who had arrested Mr. Holt and his staff in 1950. He was now a full colonel. He told us that he had been badly burned during a napalm bomb raid on Seoul and showed us his still unhealed wounds. His name was Choe. We called him "Roasted Joe." He switched on his radio. There was Western dance music.

"You like that, don't you? Will you have a drink with me? To peace."

"To peace. Let it be soon."

He left the radio on and walked out. The dance music ended and someone said: "This is the Armed Forces Network broadcasting to you from the Mark Hopkins Hotel,

San Francisco, California. In heavy fighting east and west of Seoul, United Nations forces using tanks and air support have repulsed a number of Chinese attacks; 6,000 dead were counted on the battlefield after the Reds retreated. Our troops . . ."

Roasted Joe walked in and switched off the set. This was February, 1951. So they were still fighting. But perhaps they were expecting negotiations soon, and that was why Uncle promised goat meat, electric light, a bathroom, classics, Western music, and plenty of space in our new home.

Uncle came in just then.

"I am preparing a feast for you," he said. "You will have to wait a little."

It was late in the evening and we had not eaten since the night before, but who will not wait for a feast?

It came hours later—a small finger-bowl full of mixed grain and a spoonful of boiled seaweed. How about the other promises of Uncle?

We spent the night, unable to sleep, in an unheated room. Manpo is not so cold as the Chung Kang Djin area from which we had just come. Chung Kang Djin is known as the coldest spot in Korea. Manpo, on the other hand, in the early February nights is no colder than fifty-five degrees below freezing.

We spent two nights and one day in that room, listening to Roasted Joe next door interrogating people. Once he asked us to keep quiet because they were going to read aloud to one another. Through cracks in the door, we watched. Roasted Joe had the chair. He was dictating slowly from the Cominform Journal. Around him, other officers were laboriously writing it down in longhand. The subject was the differences between various members of the central committee of the Hungarian Communist Party in 1948.

On February 5, escorted by Roasted Joe and a young sub-lieutenant nicknamed "Fatso," we walked north three miles on the ice of the Yalu river, passing under the intact international bridge, to the hamlet of Moo Yong Nee. The end house in the village had been requisitioned for us, and its inhabitants, evicted, were moving into the already over-crowded home of another farmer. The old wife of the farmer who had been turned out smiled at us and greeted us with an elaborate honorific formula. Fatso, using the lowest form, ordered her to "shut up."

All Korean farmhouses have a sunken kitchen at one end. The smoke from the hearth passes through channels under the other three rooms of the house and comes up a chimney made of a hollow tree. Thus the fuel used for cooking serves also to heat the floors of the rooms. The room nearest the kitchen is the warmest, and usually the largest. By the time the fumes reach the second room they have lost most of their heat and, in order to heat the last room, there is a firing point at the side of the house, under the wall partitioning the end room from the middle room. When we arrived at our "residence," the sergeant who had escorted us from Ha Djang Nee, and whom we had nick-named "the Voyou," was burning some twigs in the out-side hearth, to heat the middle and end rooms. The guards —Fatso, the Voyou, and Buchenwald (the kindly guard who had helped me wash at the Ministry of the Interior) —occupied the room next to the kitchen, the warmest. The end room had a hole in the wall, no paper on the door, and no straw mats on the ground, so our whole group of ten had to go into the middle room, which was nine feet by nine. It was a week before five of us could move into the end room.

The first day in our new home, no meal was served until four in the afternoon, when Fatso walked in with an enor-mous quantity of rice, pickled cabbage, and bean sprouts cooked in soy sauce. For the second time in many months we had the pleasure of feeling full. This looked good. If we were to be fed like this . . .

It turned out that, as we had had no breakfast or lunch, Fatso had decided to serve three meals in one. The next day hunger set in again. It was far less acute than at Ha Djang Nee, but it was there all the same.

We complained about the food whenever we could, to whoever came to see us. One of our visitors, a full colonel with bitter lines running down each side of his mouth, told us we should be thankful to get what we were getting. Most people in Korea, he said, did not have as much. We should not ask for more, nor was there any chance of our getting more, with the Korean conflict steadily developing

157

towards something like what was happening in Indo-China. According to the colonel, there was no chance of our getting out before the end of World War Three, and we were jolly lucky to be treated the way we were being treated.

The colonel seemed a very important person to us, accustomed as we were to receiving orders from sergeants, and we tended to believe what he told us. Our illusions about impending negotiations faded, and freedom became more remote—something no longer connected with us, something which belonged only to those pilots who flew high above us on their night patrols. They flew over us, and an hour later, they could be in a land of freedom. We were jealous of them, but we wished them good luck, just as we wished good luck to those who on March 3, 1951, dived straight into the bursts of the Chinese anti-aircraft batteries and blasted two spans of the international bridge into the river. We cheered, even though the blast tore our paper door and left us freezing for three days before the guards gave us some newspapers to keep out the Manchurian winter.

The day after the bombing, we could see thousands of Chinese civilians pouring towards the bridge from all directions. Soon large piles of big stones began mounting near the bridge, and trains unloaded cargoes of beams on the Chinese side. An elaborate structure of beams and rock went up in the middle of the river where the spans had been blasted. Ready-made steel bridge sections arrived and the night was made blue by the sparks of the welders. Above, the planes woom-woomed regularly every night. We told ourselves that as soon as the repairs were complete, the planes would come to blast the bridge once more.

Trains started rumbling over the new spans. Day after day we waited for the strike, but nothing came. We were not to know why for many days. We consoled ourselves with the thought that all the bridges between the frontier and the front were undoubtedly destroyed—for could we not hear frequent thunder of explosions in the distance? That could only be bridges being bombed. With communications made impossible, with constant pounding of the front line by air and artillery, the Communist losses, we thought, must be terrific. Surely they would not stand this pace for long. Optimism reappeared and found its expression in some drawings of nudes—charcoal pin-ups to grace our barren walls.

Fatso, our camp commandant—his real name was Pak Yong See—was very shocked. He was convinced these were drawings of Korean women—they might have been anything, for the artist had no knowledge of his art. Fatso was angry. He rubbed the nudes off the wall and then gave us a lecture, like those he gave daily to the other two guards, for Fatso, besides being camp commandant, was also the political officer. A great talker, apparently able to go on forever, he lectured his two subordinates daily from about seven in the evening till midnight. The others would

159

take down "The Word" in longhand and would study it for hours. There were monthly examinations in "political vigilance" at Manpo, and promotion depended very much on marks. The Voyou—Han Sen Cho—and a self-satisfied new arrival, O Chang Nyun (whom we nicknamed "Ernest" after Wilde's play), were ambitious.

Buchenwald could not care less. What he seemed to enjoy most was pawing the two young and plain peasant girls who cooked and carried water for us and the guards. One of those girls spat a lot. The other spent much time polishing the brass spoons of the guards with clay. We called them "Spit and Polish." But even Buchenwald had to take dictation and fill his copybook with chapter after chapter of the *Short Course in the History of the Communist Party of the Soviet Union* (Bolsheviks). The Korean edition is full of coupled Chinese characters, transliterated and therefore unintelligible, completely mysterious to peasant boys like Buchenwald.

A North Korean major who was kind to us once asked whether we understood Marx. Receiving our affirmative answer, he voiced his admiration at such erudition and admitted that, although obliged to read Marx a number of times, he had never understood what it was all about. No one can escape indoctrination.

The guards did not appear to enjoy Fatso's indoctrination sessions, and we thought that was why they liked going to Pyongyang. One of them went there once a month. The money allocated to the camp commandant for our upkeep had to be fetched from the capital monthly. There did not appear to be any branch cashier in Manpo. The round trip took three weeks on an average, sometimes more.

Every month, long before the emissary returned with the cash, Fatso would run out of money, and would have to borrow either from the village headman or the Chinese farmer who supplied us with our vegetables. Fatso could never get money without security, so each month, for a short period, his record player was taken away to the moneylender's house.

That record player was one of Uncle's promises that half materialized. It was a very old His Master's Voice model which arrived at the house one day, strapped on the back of an ox, together with a case of records. Fatso, the Voyou and Ernest were away, and only Buchenwald was there. He let us go into the guardroom and choose the records we wanted. There was Tchaikovsky's *1812 Overture,* two solos from *Boris Godunof,* sung by Chaliapin, the last movement of Beethoven's *Pastoral, La donna è mobile, Sole Mio* and *Auld Lang Syne;* the remaining records were poor Korean imitations of Japanese, Chinese, and Mongolian music.

Buchenwald, a friendly soul, placed his finger on the center of the record and made it revolve—the spring was broken. He worked us through all the Western music. It was garbled, but still agreeable. Then Fatso came. We had to leave the guardroom. Revolving the turntable with their

161

fingers, the guards tried all the records. Then, over a fire, they bent the Western ones into rough vases, bowls, "fruit baskets" and ashtrays. They gave us the Beethoven *Pastoral* ashtray for our room.

Late into the night, every night, in front of an admiring audience of village girls—whom Buchenwald surreptitiously pawed—Fatso played his records of atonal Asiatic songs, garbled by the irregularity with which the guard on duty propelled the turntable. We lay awake trying to ignore the noise.

The record player was the security against which Fatso borrowed money to keep the camp going. But besides offering security, he had to flatter the moneylenders, for they were influential members of the local Party organization who could not be bullied like the ordinary farmers. So they were frequently invited to meals. For the inhabitants of Korea, the test between good and bad food is whether it consists of rice or lower-grade cereals. Fatso's invitations were always eagerly accepted by the money lenders. For we had rice to eat, and they, it appeared, could get only mixed grains. The village headman, a young man with a pleasant disposition whom we called "Jack the Ripper" because he officiated as the village butcher, had many relatives. Two of these, his sister and his cousin, had been appointed our cooks and were eating part of our ration.

The Ripper himself was a frequent guest, bringing along his old mother and his baby son. The arrival of guests meant a sharp reduction of our ration. The level of the rice in the bowls fell catastrophically, and we made violent protests, in the presence of the guests. This by Far Eastern standards was most improper behavior, for it made Fatso lose face. He would scream back, very angrily, but beyond screaming he took no reprisals against us. He was obviously under orders not to hit us or punish us in any way without consulting his superiors, and that he could not do because his prevarications might then be exposed.

So Fatso swallowed his pride and went on robbing us, keeping us hungry, buying Chinese cigarettes for himself out of our allowance, depriving us often of a whole month's meager tobacco ration. And we went on protesting, fighting hard against the squeeze. Each protest brought a slight amelioration—a temporary one—for the next day Fatso would start his tricks again, and we would protest again. Thus, by constant struggle, we kept at a level which, while obviously lower than what the North Korean Government intended, was higher than what Fatso would have provided had he had it all his own way. Certainly, our life did not get "better and better every day" as Uncle had predicted.

Most of Uncle's promises never materialized. We never saw the goat meat or the milk, and we used to say that when electricity was installed we would be liberated.

Electricity was installed in May, 1951, but it did not bring liberation, only a radio which Fatso borrowed from the cross-eyed village schoolmistress who wanted to marry him. One day he tuned in to the United Nations broadcast in Korean. He was alone in his room and he fell asleep. The Korean broadcast ended and an American voice read out a news bulletin followed by a review of what the political commentators were saying:

"A large Chinese offensive has been repulsed. Eighty thousand Communists have been killed. When will the Reds realize there is no sense in batting their heads against a wall?"

When, oh when?

That was early May, 1951, and the swallows had just come back from the South to build a nest above our door. Then there were the pups.

The Ripper brought them one day—a little, gray, friendly creature who was going to look like an Alsatian with floppy ears and a small tubby individual with great character and a dislike for familiarity. They were called Dicky and Bouleau. They grew to love us, and to hate policemen. Dicky, a fine, huge dog with a heavy chest, would rush snarling savagely at any uniformed visitor. He did tolerate the guards, but a neighboring lieutenant with a low-slung, waddling behind and a Narcissus complex would stand away from the house screaming for help whenever he tried to visit Fatso, because Dicky would rush at him, all fangs bared. Delighted, we would restrain our pet, who would put on a big show of affection towards us, while still grumbling at the intruder.

The Communist Narcissus would quickly slip off his shoes and scuttle into the guardroom. Then Bouleau would take over. With measured dignity, he would approach this new footwear and remove it to a secluded corner, where he would calmly chew it to ribbons under our admiring glances.

The guards would have disposed of our pets had it not been for "Alfred." Alfred was a North Korean police major who had something to do—we never knew quite what—with the administration of our camp. He requisitioned a room in the Ripper's house and spent long hours basking in the sun, occasionally going to Manpo with his map case. He was very polite, even pleasant, and was always willing to commiserate with us on our plight. He had been an ordinary coolie before the war, and had been imprisoned by the Japanese for Communist activities. After 1945, he had gone to school, joined the police, and finally become a major. We did not think he would get much higher because he lacked the puritanical streak characteristic of the ambitious Communist official. Alfred was not a fanatic. He sat in the sun with his Korean copy of Stalin's *Questions of Leninism* and fell asleep, always halfway down the first page. In the company of our doctor, he frequently got drunk, and ran a number of affairs with some Korean policewomen until Mrs. Alfred appeared on the scene.

He had told me he had lost trace of his wife in the war, and that he had had no news of his family since 1950. That was in answer to one of my frequent protests against the lack of correspondence. But if he did not know where his wife was, she obviously knew where he was, for one day she turned up dressed in colorful fineries, with their two little sons in neat sailor costumes.

The children of the village, skinny and dirty in their rags, were very antagonistic to these well-dressed, well-fed newcomers, and Alfred's children, who took to Perruche—as everyone else did—would run to him for protection.

Alfred had to reduce his drinking somewhat. But his wife dropped her fineries, and—dressed like her sisters, the village women—started her endless round of water-carrying, fire-lighting, cooking, wood-chopping, field-cultivating, and pig-feeding. Soon she was pregnant. She had arrived smiling, looking rather frail and interesting in her bright silks. A few months later, her fineries were locked away in some chest, her belly was distended, her features had grown coarse and the lines multiplied daily on her face.

Alfred continued to fall asleep in the sun halfway down the first page of Stalin's *Questions of Leninism*. He was not a hard man, but like all other Koreans he had not taken the "emancipation of women" to heart, and he continued to treat his wife like a child-bearing beast of burden, designed for those low menial tasks that are beneath the dignity of the Korean male. But he was not a bad man. One night, early in July, he offered us some rice spirits. He had a guest, a captain, and they were getting drunk at our house, away from Mrs. Alfred. The guest, reeling amiably, approached us and told us that negotiations had started between the United Nations and the Communists. We were mad with joy; then we began to fear a disappointment, and we told ourselves—trying hard to make it convincing—that these negotiations were bound to fail, that even if they produced results it would take months, that the problems facing the negotiators were almost insoluble.

But we did not believe ourselves.

We tackled Alfred on the subject the next day. He was surprised. He had not intended to tell us, obviously. He and Fatso had pursued a consistent policy of keeping us ignorant of all news. Still, we knew, and reluctantly he gave us some detail. His reaction to this news was identical with ours. He desperately wanted the talks to be successful, but like us he was afraid of disappointment and he repeated all the reasons we had given ourselves for not hoping.

But, he too, did not believe himself.

Taking advantage of this, the French managed to sell a prized piece of jewelry belonging to Madame Martel, seventy-six-year-old mother of Charles Martel, the Chancellor of their Legation in Seoul. With the proceeds they gave a Quatorze Juillet reception. By some magic the shabby, filthy room had been transformed into a French *salon*. In his rags, Georges Perruche managed somehow to look as debonair, charming, gay, as if he were wearing tails. The sickening rice spirit, handed round in aluminum bowls with some inimitably French remark, sparkled al-

167

most like champagne. For a little while the magic of these Frenchmen took us out of captivity. They managed to produce remarks we had not heard before, to tell new stories, to make us feel that they were not the people with whom we daily shared the cattle turnips, but the French Legation having us as guests. We went back to our room —the English room—which the French called *la Chambre des Lords,* treasuring the beautifully handwritten invitation cards beginning:

M. GEORGES PERRUCHE

Déchargé d'Affaires,

etc.

Fatso, Ernest, and the Voyou had waited on us at the party, bringing special dishes cooked for us by Mrs. Alfred herself. Her husband was hopelessly drunk under the table. We ate real meat for the first time in many months. There was a meat ration for us once a month, and Fatso normally bought a small pig with the money sent to him from the capital. The beast was killed by the Voyou, who knelt on the quivering body while the blood flowed out of the carotid arteries he had cut with a blunt knife. The Ripper dressed the carcass, and the choice pieces were sold by Fatso to the village. He and the guards ate hams. To us they gave intestines, insufficiently washed, half-cooked. Not everyone would eat them.

One night, when Owen and I were sitting in the courtyard, unable to sleep because of the stifling atmosphere

in our room, Buchenwald went to the kitchen, and out of
the pot where the guards' food was kept he brought us a
choice piece of meat, over a pound in weight. Thanking
him profusely, we went back and shared our prize. We sat
up munching. Some weeks before, the guards had cooked
their meat in our turnip pot and they had left a marrow-
bone there, which we later found. Not one of us could bear
to give it up, and we had to cut for it with our home-made
pack of cards. The one who won broke it between two
stones, and the rest of us walked away because we could
not watch.

We were hungry, and we protested, holding endless
conferences with Fatso, who insisted on being approached
by an elected "leader." We did not want a leader, arguing
that a small group like ours did not need rule. We could
decide by discussion—we claimed—and having a leader
or spokesman would create a need for more uniformity.
This we wanted to avoid. Moreover, it must be said, although we always presented a united front to the authorities we had such differences of opinions and tastes that
leadership was impossible. Not one of us felt capable of
undertaking the job. This, to Fatso, trained in deep respect
of hierarchy, was sheer heresy—and very inconvenient to
boot, because he could never approach us as a group, if
that did not suit our purpose.

One such occasion was when Fatso wanted us to dig
silos to store our winter vegetables. He marked out on the
ground two huge squares twenty-five feet on a side, and

told us to dig eight feet deep. The cold was beginning to set in, and our ragged footwear was not up to such labor. Some of us who believed fanatically in exercise—even when there was not enough to eat—declared that we were going to dig for our own amusement, and promised not to criticize those who abstained on the grounds that Fatso would have to feed us whether we dug silos or not. This attitude, which obliged the guards themselves to work, drove them crazy. They appealed, shouted, bullied, cajoled, but nothing happened. Ernest tried ordering Owen:

"Go and dig."

"Is it obligatory or is it voluntary?"

"It is not your business to know."

"Then it is not my business to dig."

"All right, it is voluntary."

"Then I do not want to dig."

"But it is essential to dig the silos so that we can feed you in the winter."

"If it is essential," said Owen, walking away, "then you will get it done without our help."

We were not strong enough for digging, and those who tried it were taken ill. They caught colds, had bouts of malaria, and fits of utter exhaustion.

The vinous doctor, who came to see us whenever it was necessary, stethoscoped us and assured us solemnly that we were being grossly underfed. He would protest to the appropriate authorities, he said. Meanwhile, how about some calcium injections? And some penicillin just in case?

Atabrine? Only one tablet per malaria patient per day—
he had no more, but as soon as a consignment arrived he
would see what he could do. Meanwhile, could he palpate
our spleens? He warmed his hands before touching us,
warmed the stethoscope, spoke in a quiet gentle voice and
was always sympathetic. He tried us with all the drugs the
Russians gave him, including a polyvaccine whose pros-
pectus claimed that it not only prevented typhus, typhoid,
tetanus, cholera and encephalitis, but also phlebitis, ar-
teriosclerosis, fibrositis, and a long list of other diseases
with unknown Russian names. We were very ill for two
weeks, unable to move our arms. The guards, who also had
been treated, lay moaning on the floor of their room. The
two little cooks, Spit and Polish, had been injected too, but
they could not rest. They went on carrying water, chop-
ping wood, lighting fires, laundering for the guards and
running errands. We saw them weeping with pain, but still
they had to work.

CHAPTER ·8

Brain Wash

As THE weather grew warmer, we lay on our backs, driven by boredom to the umpteenth reading of Communist books with which we were provided. Besides the so-called "Communist classics"—works of Marx, Engels, Lenin, and Stalin—we occasionally had modern Russian novels, magazines, and newspapers, which concentrated on proving that all was wrong with the West, and that only the East was capable of giving the human being a chance. Every bad aspect of our civilization was pounced upon, mounted on a pedestal of words, spotlighted, magnified, analyzed. No good side was ever mentioned. England, said one of the books, was like a pond of stagnant, fetid water where nothing lived, where all was stifled by the green slime on the surface. America was America as seen by one who searched only for horror, soullessness, and filth. France, as painted by Ilya Ehrenbourg, was a decadent caricature of her great past. Her art, her letters, the wit of her people were all replaced now, according to the Soviet books, by slavish bootlicking, by sickening subservience to

172

American dictate, by a sordid desire for moneymaking at all costs. The Western world was decaying, wrote the Soviet books. Whole forests must have gone to print this sentence the billions of times it has been printed by Soviet presses. In most cases this propaganda was ham-fisted, lacking the subtle strokes that go home. But there were some of those strokes, springing from well-known, undeniable defects of our system, and hitting straight at the conscience of the reader.

And there was the mass—the overwhelming mass—of words following one another towards the same goal. It was not indoctrination by an interlocutor who irritates and whose arguments goad one to refute. It was endless repetition—a monotonous and single-minded repetition which, unopposed by what the French call "*un autre son de cloche,*" began to make an impression.

There came a time when I had to stop reading those books, to stop practicing Russian because with the study of language the absurd and constant assertion began to leave its mark, began to find an echo, and I felt my thinking processes becoming tangled, my critical faculties blunted. I could not think, and I was afraid. There is nothing more frightening than a book expressing thought for a man who cannot think. It does not matter what the thought is. Its quality is beside the point. If you cannot think, it frightens you by its immense repetition, just as the immense repetition of the ocean swell frightens the shipwrecked nonswimmer.

173

Then they made a mistake. They gave us Robert Louis Stevenson's "Treasure Island" in English, and I read it fourteen times in succession, casting off the world of Capitalism, Socialism, Communism, Stakhanovism, and plunging desperately into that forgotten world of a child's imagination, with pirates and treasure and overworked clichés. I recaptured my childhood, then my youth, the books I had read, the men I had known, the power to think. I could read Marx again, and question myself honestly without fear.

Robert Louis Stevenson made us lighthearted, so we started dancing lessons. Those of us who could dance taught those who couldn't. Music was home-made—singing and beating a box to keep time. The guards were very interested, and the two young cooks were even more interested. They watched, giggling, while a diplomat and a journalist, in cast-off rags, pirouetted solemnly to the tune of a French waltz. Later, behind the house, we surprised Spit and Polish trying to duplicate our steps.

The weather was fine, it was not cold, and we were therefore less hungry. With a conscious effort we pushed thoughts of our families out of our minds—it was easier that way. On August 2, 1951, an official of the North Korean Ministry for Foreign Affairs came to visit us. He said that in the evening he would make an important pronouncement. We waited six hours while he fed and rested. At eight o'clock he told us officially that "a message had been received" from our families. "They were all well and were thinking of us."

To all our questions he answered that he was not authorized to say more. He added, however, that we could write short messages to our families, which would be transmitted. We did not really believe him, but then we could find no good reason for a lie on his part. Why should he tell us we could write to our families if he had no intention of forwarding the messages? Why come all the way from Pyongyang, as he said he had, to do that?

It was incredibly difficult writing those messages. What can you say after a complete year without news? What can you say to an almost total stranger who for months and months has lived a life independent from yours? How can you escape banality? How can you write something useful? Something that might reestablish that contact which perhaps has been broken by separation?

Captain Holt, who is unmarried, asked whether he could write an order for his bank to pay some money to his sister. Permission was granted, and one of us wrote in block letters for Captain Holt, whose eyesight had badly deteriorated:

TO WESTMINSTER BANK, COVENT GARDEN: PLEASE GIVE MY SISTER FIFTY POUNDS FOR THEATRE TICKETS.

Captain Holt signed the message. And, with those the rest of us sent, it was received in Whitehall by Mr. R. H.

Scott, then in charge of Far Eastern affairs at the Foreign Office.

Fifty pounds for theatre tickets! Surely one does not give fifty pounds for theatre tickets? At ten shillings a ticket it makes one hundred performances, or fifty at a pound a ticket. Whitehall (we learned after our release) was concerned. Surely there must be something more to this message?

Graphologists were consulted (we did not hear of this, of course, until after our release). Yes, the message proper was not written by the person who signed. The nib that had been used was different. The ink had come from a different bottle. Whose was the handwriting of the message proper?

Prolonged tests established beyond a doubt that the message proper had been written by me. The signature was compared with signatures of Captain Holt in the Foreign Office files. There were slight differences. Was it a genuine signature, or a forgery? A majority decision established the genuineness of the signature. All right— what did the message mean? The specialists in cryptography got the message. They worked and worked, then gave up. The paper was tested for invisible ink. It was X-rayed, photographed with infrared and ultraviolet, soaked in chemicals, tested for smell, taste, color.

In desperation, the Foreign Office finally consulted Captain Holt's bank. "Oh no," said the bank, "there's nothing unusual about the message. Captain Holt frequently

sends us orders of this kind. He has an account with Keith
Prowse for his sister to buy theatre tickets, and he au-
thorizes us occasionally to pay some money into that account. No, there is nothing unusual about that message.
We do not think there is any secret meaning attached to
this."

There wasn't. But the sending of the messages had un-
settled us, and it took us over two months to recover our
vegetative frame of mind, only to be disturbed again by
the arrival of a Korean who said he was the Communists'
"plenipotentiary for prisoner questions." He talked to us
through an English-speaking Russian. This Korean repeated to Captain Holt and to me the statement of the
Minister of the Interior to the effect that North Korea had
counterattacked on June 26 to put an end to South Korean
provocation. After a couple of interviews the Korean disappeared and we were left in the care of the Russian. He
wanted our biographies. Then he wanted to talk politics.

"Can't you see," he asked, "that the capitalist world
wants war, while we want peace? Don't you realize that
the United States, Britain, and France are preparing a
third world war, increasing war production, building war
plants and atom-bomb factories while Russia is building
works of peace—canals, hydroelectric stations, universities?"

"Do you consider France, or rather the French Union,
as a fairly representative state of what you call the capitalist world?"

177

"What are you driving at?"

"I've asked you a question."

"All right, let's admit that France is a fairly representative state of the capitalist world."

"According to figures printed in your magazine *New Times*, for each one of the inhabitants of the French Union, thirty-five United States dollars are spent every year on armaments. . . . All right," said our Russian, "Don't you think that is an enormous sum to spend for every man, woman and child?"

"According to figures printed in another issue of the same magazine, the U.S.S.R. budget includes a total expenditure for 'nonpeaceful purposes' of two hundred United States dollars per head, per year. Don't you think that is an enormous sum to spend for every man, woman and child?"

"You are juggling with figures. The comparison is unfair. You take France to compare with the U.S.S.R. Why do you not take America? America is spending far more. I can show you figures tomorrow that will prove to you America spends enormous sums on armaments; and all her satellites also spend enormous sums. I will show you the figures tomorrow."

"I'll be glad to get them. After I divide them by two, they will be very interesting."

"Why do you say after you divide them by two?"

"Because when talking of American expenditure on armaments your publications always double the figure.

They mention the expenditure once as it is voted in the
U.S.A. for military aid to other countries, then your publications mention that very same military aid once more as
armament expenditure of the countries receiving American aid. One and the same sum of money is added to itself
and therefore doubled. Moreover, when you speak of
American war expenditure, you include in that all investments in heavy industry, whereas such investments in the
Soviet Union are called 'peaceful building.'"

"But haven't you seen what percentage of the total
budget military expenditure represents in France and
what percentage in the Soviet Union? French military
expenditure is over fifty percent. Ours is not thirty percent.
The U.S.S.R. is a huge country with huge frontiers to defend."

"Against the Chinese Communists, for instance? And as
for your percentages, that is real juggling with figures. The
Western economies are economies where private enter-
prise still prevails. Wholesale and retail trade, much of
industry, whole branches of transport are administered by
private individuals, and are not included in the Governmental budget, whereas in Russia everything appears on
the budget, down to the estimates for repainting news-
stands. As a result your total budget figures are much
larger, and enormous military expenditure, expressed as
percentages of the total budget figures, can be made to
look smaller than the corresponding, and in reality smaller,
Western figures. All your articles on economics are worked

on that basis. You boast of low direct taxation—10% as compared with 50% in Britain. But in the U.S.S.R. the State owns all the production facilities. It is the universal boss, the supreme monopoly, and it fixes prices where it likes, getting all its revenue from sales—from indirect taxation in other words. I don't know why you bother with direct taxation even."

"All these statistics are beside the point. The fact remains that capitalism needs war and Communism needs peace. Why should we bother to have a war? The capitalist world of today was built up on a system of colonial exploitation and of foreign markets and raw material sources. The big industrial countries of the West imported raw materials from the backward countries—including their colonies—and exported finished products at tremendous profits. Before the first world war the main markets for the capitalist countries were Russia, Eastern Europe, China, South-East Asia, and South America. After the first world war Russia dropped out of the capitalist market. After the second world war Eastern Europe and China dropped out. The struggle of the colonial peoples for national independence is further restricting the capitalists' market. The colonial people want to develop their own economies. Having suffered from long imperialist oppresson, and inspired by the example of Democratic China, the people of South-East Asia will soon leave the capitalist world market and join the people's democratic world market. India will join us soon. How long do you think the Indian peasant

180

will stand for exploitation through six stages of middle-men, when he knows that his brother the Chinese peasant is no longer exploited? You will lose India. Lenin said that the battle between capitalism and Communism will defi-nitely turn in favor of the latter when Russia, China, and India have been wrested from the capitalists. Russia and China are gone. India is going. What will happen then in the capitalist world? Ever-expanding production, ever-contracting markets. Crisis of overproduction. The small will fall, and will be driven by despair to see the light and join us. One by one the countries of the capitalist world, ruined by competition for markets, will fall into our arms. And then the United States will remain alone against the rest of mankind. This is the inevitable course of history, and you can do nothing about it, because the capitalist, egged on by the urge for profit, never bothers to develop the purchasing power of his markets. You are not develop-ing Africa and South America as markets. You are reduc-ing the purchasing power of those continents, and you will pay for that with the loss of the smaller capitalist coun-tries."

"The trouble with you is that you think in terms of theory—Marxist theory—and not reality. There are states-men in the West fully conscious of the changes now taking place all over the world, and they are shaping their policy accordingly."

"They will not succeed, and we will win, without resort-ing to war."

"If by that you mean that the West might give you victory by making unpardonable mistakes, I agree. But what will happen if the West does not make those mistakes? Won't you then resort to what you call a just war for the establishment of socialism in another country?"

"You do not understand," said the Russian, and sent me home. The next day he left politics for philosophy, and found himself in very deep water with Jean Meadmore, who outquoted him on Engels, Marx, and Stalin. Then he asked for dissertations on the various countries we had served in. Captain Holt, who is an Arab expert, gave him highly technical details on camel-riding, Arab calligraphy, and the relative merits of the Iraqi Army and Police polo teams. The Russian interrogator seemed slightly disconcerted.

He tried George Blake, the British vice-consul, on Holland, and received an erudite paper on Franz Hals.

From me he wanted something on Greece, especially the Communist problem. I told him that really to understand this problem one had to go back to ancient Greece, that one had to have a short historical review. "Of course, of course," he said.

He kept me for five days. After the seventy-second manuscript page, when he saw that I was still dealing with the Iconoclast-Iconolater feud in Tenth-Century Byzantium, he gave up and sent for the next internee.

Perruche really solved matters by telling the Russian some of his stories. After that we never looked back. The

Russian gave up talking Marxism and brought us vodka; our conversations would not bear repeating. I confess that on one occasion, arms around one another, we sang the *Internationale,* followed by "Caviar comes from virgin sturgeon."

After our singsong, followed at a respectful distance by my apprehensive guard (Ernest's sense of what was proper must have been strained that day) the Russian indoctrinator and I went for a walk around Manpo. There wasn't much to see, but the Russian wanted to show me where he lived. When we reached the river bank, he explained how every morning he'd come out from his house in a pair of running shorts and slippers, do calisthenics in front of the admiring populace, then splash himself from the small channel where water still flowed between the slabs of ice. He was proud of the fact that a group of young Koreans had taken to joining him in the morning. After his exercises, he would drink "gallons of milk." He advised me to follow his example, thus building up my resistance against the cold. I told him that such early-morning energy was perhaps possible when one could drink "gallons of milk," but quite out of the question on a diet of boiled turnips. Kuzma Kuzmich expressed his surprise at the absence of milk from our diet. There was a lot of milk in Manpo, according to him.

We had nicknamed him Kuzma Kuzmich after a character who reappears regularly in every new Soviet novel— the convert to Communism who still suffers from "survivals of capitalism." Our Kuzma Kuzmich, a White Russian from Harbin who had taken up the "faith" in 1945, was not always successful in expressing the fanaticism expected of neophytes. He would speak longingly of "business," and his eyes would light up so, when told of cabarets in Alexandria or of Beirut dives. Moreover, although he had read Comrade Stalin's famous treatise on nationalities, Kuzma Kuzmich suffered from a racial-superiority complex. He treated the Koreans' deference as something naturally due to him. And when he spoke to us of "the yellows" there was much of the "old imperialist Chinahand" in his tone of voice. He was, however, very condescending in answering the salutes of Korean officers, for they all saluted us in the streets—two salutes, one for Kuzma and one for me. I tried to imitate Kuzma's offhand nod, pleasantly conscious of Ernest's discomfiture some paces behind, and wondering how the Korean officers, who had saluted me, felt when told by Ernest who I was.

Outside Kuzma's house, there was a group of North Korean amputees from the nearby hospital. They called Kuzma "tovarishch" and offered their hands. Kuzma shook them condescendingly. One of the mutilated men spoke some Russian and he began haranguing Kuzma, thanking him for having come to help the Koreans against Anglo-American imperialism. Kuzma replied in a few words, introduced me as his tovarishch, and said I was going to speak too. Those members of the audience who could, clapped hands. Following the fashion established by Stalin, I also applauded myself.

With the "Russian-speaking" Korean as a very imaginative interpreter, I delivered a speech on the necessity for peace and an immediate release of the P.O.W.'s and internees in North Korea. To make sure my audience understood me, I frequently employed the word peace in Korean, drawing acclamations each time. To finish, I called for ten thousand cheers for peace. Ernest tried to butt in just then for the umpteenth time, and was again roundly told off by Kuzma, who did not want his demonstrations spoiled. I shook hands with the wounded, took my leave from Kuzma, and made for home in the company of my impotently raging guard. Ernest had orders to control himself, and he was obeying his orders in a commendable manner, confining himself to violent invective in the honorific form. He was very angry. With the help of a Russian, I had defied Ernest's authority. That is why he made me move on without talking, when I suddenly encountered Commissioner Lord while returning from my "peace rally."

"Deane!" the Commissioner exclaimed, a smile of joyous greeting on his face. "Well I'll be . . ." and he caught himself just in time.

"Commissioner! Well I'll be . . ." and I did not catch myself in time. With that we were separated. It was nice to know the Commissioner was still alive. Months later I learned what had happened to the missionaries after our "special group" of diplomats and journalists had left the death camp at Ha Djang Nee.

On the day we left, February 2, 1951, a new commandant had taken over from the Tiger. This new man, in the words of Commissioner Lord, was "a perfect gentleman." Brutality ceased. Many of the Tiger's prison wardens left and were replaced by new ones who were generally more considerate. Supply difficulties continued, and drugs were still short, but the internees and P.O.W.'s had the impression that this was not due to negligence on the part of the camp commandant. He himself suffered from advanced tuberculosis and could not get any streptomycin.

The tall captain who had been the Tiger's second in command and political officer disappeared and a rumor spread that he had been jailed for embezzling the P.O.W. rations. The rations, nevertheless, did not improve and the death rate remained very high. Strict orders were given that no one should be allowed to keep a check on the total number of prisoners. The Viennese Dr. Kisch died of general debility. One day twelve G.I.'s had to be buried. That seems to have been the turning point. Abruptly, as it happens in Korea, the winter ended and the hot spring was there. The death rate dropped.

The new commandant moved the camp back to Chung Kang Djin, seven miles south, in a school building near a small tributary of the Yalu. There wasn't much food, or drugs, but there was sunshine, a swimming hole, and the possibility of washing one's clothes. Even without soap, water will keep the vermin down. People became healthier, more spirited, more independent, and therefore more troublesome for this new set of guards who were under orders not to use violence. Some faults of the old regime remained, however—physical training in the mornings, for instance. The P.O.W.'s had to get up early for exercise. The civilian internees had been given up as hopeless. One morning a new guard tried to enforce his authority by having everyone turn out for calisthenics. He managed to get the occupants of one room out, then went into the other room. When he came into the courtyard again he found that those he had roused first had disappeared. He played hide and seek with the internees from room to room, until, exasperated, he unlimbered his rifle, loaded it, and said he would shoot if disobedience did not stop at once.

One of the mothers paraded her small children in single file before the guard.

"Shoot," she told him, "shoot. With one bullet you can kill three babies who are too hungry to go out and do your exercises."

The muzzle drooped and drooped. The new commandant came on the scene. He was surrounded by wailing women who complained of the guard's brutality. The commandant did not like making his subordinate lose face, but what was he to do? He did not have the Tiger's propensity for kicking women into silence. Completely unnerved by the sobs of the frightened children, the commandant publicly reprimanded his guard, and ordered that the internees should not do physical training. He left, remarking that the internees were "very difficult problem."

This man, the camp commandant, who was not unkind, had spent many years of his life learning in Communist textbooks that the West is hateful, that religion and its ministers are an imperialist tool for the oppression of the backward people. He had read almost daily in his newspapers about missionaries who "were really spies." The countrymen of these people he was administering were raining death on his own people. He had lost his family in air raids. His newspaper—which to him, a Communist, was the text of the daily lesson from his gospel—was describing Westerners as monsters. Posters stared at him from the walls caricaturing the Occidentals as sinister, bloodstained, murderous insects. Moreover, as a member of the prison administration, he was used to the straightforward Far Eastern method of dealing with the jail inmate—you treat him like an object with no personality and no opinion on any matter, an object that does what you command when you command, that never argues, that can be spoken to harshly, that would never dare importune you with requests or wails; an object that is definitely subordinate to you in every way, and whose satisfaction, bodily and spiritual, is secondary to yours, an object that would not presume to have an opinion about its guards.

188

This man, the camp commandant, with his background, was sent to a death camp with strict orders to treat "the ravishers of Korea" decently, to be kind to the missionaries "who were an imperialist tool for the oppression of backward people and were really spies." He had instructions to treat humanely those very soldiers who had "come to rend Korea apart," and to treat them humanely even when they endeavored to break his every regulation. He had to do all this, and meanwhile he had to read his newspaper which continued to describe the Occidentals—all Occidentals who were not Communists or signatories of the Stockholm peace appeal—as monstrous murderers. And he had been definitely told that he should make a good impression on his prisoners, that he should show them the superiority of the Communist world outlook over the Western world outlook.

He had to do all this while his requests for extra supplies, clothes, and medicine were refused, while thousands of trucks carrying these very things passed daily before the eyes of the people who were dying under his administration, dying for lack of the supplies, clothes, and medicine transported by the trucks a thousand yards away.

What is more, he had to explain this complex situation to his guards, who were far less complex than he was. It is hard to say whether this situation was more difficult for the commandant, who could perhaps experience doubt, or for the peasant boys who served under him and who were capable of an act of complete faith in this new religion

189

which had taught them to read and speak those long, complicated, and not always understandable words.

The commandant and his staff had to resolve the problem which faces the highly trained psychologists who run the modern Western prisons—how to be kind to a man against whom you are committing the cruelty of incarceration. I was not there to tell whether the commandant succeeded, but Bishop Cooper and Commissioner Lord, when questioned about him, gave the typical British answer:

"That commandant was a born gentleman."

If that means he succeeded in his task, then the reasons why he succeeded should be investigated. They might help us understand some of the Communist successes in Asia.

Some days before the arrival of the new commandant an elderly captain had joined the staff of the camp. He spoke good English and had been Dean of the Teachers' College in Seoul under Syngman Rhee. He told me he had left South Korea long before the war started, because he could not stand the rottenness of the administration there, and for other reasons also:

"I have many American and English friends in the South, people I respect, with decent ideas and sentiments. But there were others who would turn anyone against them—the one, for instance, who wrote outside the American P.X. in Seoul, 'No dogs—No Koreans.' And those who acted as if we had the plague when we went near them.

They called us 'dirty yellow bastards' to our faces. You have many fine ideas, many wonderful philosophies of kindness and justice. You have Christianity—I was a Christian myself—the Greek thinkers, and all the great literature which has expressed these ideas so beautifully. Intellectually, Western thought appeals more to me than Marxism-Leninism, but the people nurtured by Western thought want to, and can, call me a 'dirty yellow bastard,' while those nurtured by Marxism-Leninism are not allowed to call me that. I am a small man and I have my weaknesses. I cannot disregard insults, nor can I soften them by saying to myself, as Christ did, 'they know not what they do.'

"I prefer not to be insulted, not to be treated with contempt because my skin is a different color from yours. I believe the Russians have educated racism out of their people. And even if they have not really uprooted it, they forbid their people to insult the so-called inferior races. As a member of a so-called inferior race, which for various reasons did not develop a mechanical civilization comparable to the Western, I am bound to prefer a system that does not penalize me for something I cannot help. You say the Russians are exploiting us, making us fight their battles, that the independence they claim they gave us is pretense; but then the independence you claim you gave South Korea is also pretense. The Russian pretense is cleverer. If we are to have pretense, let us have the one that is cleverer.

"Here in North Korea the Russians mixed freely with us, and yet they did not behave indecently with our women as your troops did in the South. They let us go into their clubs and their houses to eat their food, and they came into ours, squatted on the floor with us and ate our food. They walked in the streets beside us, and when they drove they did not run us down, as your troops did, with the same contempt with which they would run over a chicken. They gave us lifts. They took us into the cabs of their trucks and let us joke with them. Even their great officials and their wives would walk in our streets and let us talk to them or shake their hands. In the South, there are Christian missionaries who go to evangelize in their huge cars. They never reach the hearts of the people because the people live in streets too narrow for the Yankee cars. The Russians walk. And they don't make us feel they are everywhere. They do not throw their weight around. They keep to their houses a lot, and when they come out they are pleasant.

"Your ideas appeal more to me than Marxism-Leninism, but I am human and I judge people by their behavior without always bothering about its motives. After all, why look a gift horse in the mouth? And I have studied your ideas for many years, so I have admiration for the West, and can put something to your credit as balance for what is to your debit. What about the peasant and the worker? They have only behavior to judge by. They can only come into contact with the man who walks into their narrow street. The overfed man in the shiny sedan is of another world."

This mild elderly man was the commandant's liaison officer with the civilian internees.

"Please," he would plead, "please do as we tell you. We have to make regulations for your own good. We do not want to be angry with you. Please do not make our job difficult. We cannot treat you properly. We are such a poor country. The poorest country in the world."

And he would give the missionaries some Communist literature to read; deliver, without conviction, little set propaganda lectures; ask for comments, accept their un-equivocal replies, and depart rather tired, smiling vaguely:

"So long, folks."

The missionaries were sorry to see the last of this man, when they moved to Manpo in October 1951, and came under the prison governor. They were told they would be in the prison, but they were also assured that the author-ities did not consider them as prisoners.

The prison consisted of dugouts bored into the side of a hill. It was officially called the House of Culture. The prisoners, instead of broad arrows, had the Chinese char-acter for culture painted on their backs. I am told they preferred it that way. What you call things is very impor-tant in the Far East. A prison that is called a prison is a far worse place to be in than a prison called a house of cul-ture, even though the two establishments might be com-pletely identical. The Far Easterner is more sensitive to

193

the meaning of words than we are. We use them much more in print and we abuse them. We juggle with them and twist them into jargon. In the Far East this process is still in its infancy, and words retain much of their magic power. They open doors, like "sesame."

The kind new commandant in Ha Djang Nee, when he took over, posted an order on the camp's bulletin board that the P.O.W.'s were no longer P.O.W.'s but brother soldiers liberated from the oppression of the capitalists. The camp he renamed: "The Camp of the Liberated American Troops." Even the attitude of the guards who had run the camp under the Tiger changed. I suspect that when the Tiger told us, during the Death March, that the executed stragglers had been put into People's Hospitals, he was trying to use the magic of words to soften the blows he was administering—to soften their impact on us, and on his own conscience. Children understand this. They call it "let's pretend," and for them it works.

Except for its name, the Manpo house of culture was an extremely harsh place. The dugouts were not heated, and the food was very scarce. The prisoners had to do heavy manual labor, and there was a high mortality rate. Only the dugout of the "missionary internees" was heated, for they were not prisoners but "protected persons." They, of course, soon disorganized the prison. The women and the children disregarded all rules, and the guards, who had orders to protect them, were driven to distraction. So the missionaries were taken out of the prison compound and billeted in some nearby houses. Unlike us they were not living as internees any more, but as people under forced residence. They could wander away for miles into the hills to cut their own firewood, and they were guarded by a sub-lieutenant who for twenty days out of each month would be away on his trip to and from the capital to bring funds. If they wanted anything during his absence, they had to go down to the prison and ask for the governor's assistance.

Once, the sub-lieutenant himself had to ask for the prison governor's assistance. Things were getting out of hand. One of the interned women—not a missionary, we shall call her A—had fallen in love with one of the men, whom we shall call B. B was not interested. A resorted to "let's pretend" and soon convinced herself that her love would have been reciprocated from the first had it not been for the interference of another man, C, who, she thought, stopped B from showing her his love. So one day she picked up a kitchen knife and tried to kill C, who stood between her and happiness. Restraining her was a noisy business. The sub-lieutenant heard it and, because he did not know how to deal with it, he appealed to the prison governor.

This high official heard the evidence, and gave his verdict.

"You," he said to B, "must be conscious of your responsibility. You have aroused desire in this woman, and you are driving her mad. She is losing her sanity through wanting

195

you. That is a terrible thing you are doing to her. Why don't you sleep with her? That will cure her and make life easier for everybody. It is very troublesome for me. You say you are married; but your wife is not here. She would not know. Be a good fellow."

The major's solution was not adopted, and the woman had to be given solitary confinement after another attempt at murder. She became less violent.

That was the only case of punishment, and the other internees were glad it was administered. For lighter offenses, such as breaking bounds, black-marketing, going to the movies in town, getting uproariously drunk with the locals, only reprimands were administered.

CHAPTER 9

Pyongyang

THE day of my "peace rally," Kuzma Kuzmich revealed great news: "On November 27, 1951, at the cease-fire negotiations, agreement was reached on a demarcation line, and a time limit was set for the discussion and settlement of all outstanding questions. Everything is to be settled by December 27, 1951."

Our minds, starved of any news, pounced on this fragment of information, worried it, and built out of it countless reconstructions of what "must have happened" and what was "bound to happen." The diplomats of the group trotted out precedents, quoted from past treaties. Discussions developed into arguments and senseless quarrels. We emerged from these with a sense of shame and often thanks only to the superbly detached logic of Captain Holt. Though it cost him an effort, he could be dispassionate about a subject which affected him vitally. He kept his good-mannered patience even in the face of rude, unjustified abuse.

The news which Kuzma told us in the days that followed proved how right Captain Holt was. It was almost worrying to think of the uncanny precision with which this trained diplomat, on the basis of such flimsy information, could predict the snags that were cropping up.

We went through another period of agonizing emotional ups and downs, from which most of us took refuge in stubborn pessimism. Shattered hopes of liberty are hard to bear for the prisoner. Thus it was with a carefully studied unconcern that we greeted the arrival of a polite North Korean major who made us fill forms, printed in English, about our identities and past history. The major spent the night with us. Just after we had bedded down, Fatso, our camp commandant, announced that M. Chanteloup, the interned correspondent of Agence France Presse, and myself were leaving in the morning for the North Korean capital.

"It's the twenty-eighth of December," we reasoned. "They probably want to make a New Year propaganda broadcast to prove they treat prisoners well. They are going to take us to Pyongyang for a third degree. They'll try to make us talk on the radio."

We were driven most of the way in a jeep, escorted by an unusually solicitous Fatso and two police sergeants who were very uncomfortable trying to stay in the bouncing jeep without inconveniencing us. Fortunately, since it was the coldest period of the year, the journey took less than twenty hours. This was possible because all the bridges were in working order, and there were very many

198

bridges—both road and rail. Over them, even in daylight, flowed a stream of traffic. What then, had been those noises of bombing we had so frequently heard? What had been bombed? Not one in ten of the bridges had ever been hit, and even the damaged ones were repaired. Not one of the numerous tunnels was caved in. What had the United Nations army engineers done during the retreat? Here and there, on the road, lay the corroding remains of a Sherman tank.

Aside from the bridges, we saw such destruction as I had not seen even in Kiel or Hamburg. Of course, the Korean buildings are more vulnerable. They collapse more easily than European reinforced-concrete structures, and they collapse almost completely, their earthen walls leaving no trace on the earth to which they crash.

We arrived at the Ministry of the Interior in Pyongyang at four o'clock in the morning December 31, 1951. We were not expected. The orderly officer, a quietly spoken captain with an excellent command of Japanese, tried to make us comfortable, but he had only hard chairs to offer and his floor was not designed for sleeping, unlike normal Korean floors. People walked on it without removing their shoes and spat on it. Some other officers assembled to view the new arrivals.

"Why do you think you have been brought here? Don't you think that if we wanted a broadcast from you we could record it at Manpo? If it were an interrogation, we could have carried it out in Manpo. Anyhow, after eighteen months of internment you haven't got anything to say which might be of interest to us. No, you are very lucky. You will hear very good things soon."

The next morning a Russian-speaking captain came to see us.

"The war," he said, "will finish quickly, and you will go home."

Two majors were turned out of the room which they used as office and bedchamber. We were given their beds and two blankets. A stove was fitted and the two guards appointed to look after us stoked it day and night. This was welcome because of the cold, but also a nuisance because the occupants of the other offices in the building, who had enough coal only for four hours every day, came to our room for heat, whenever they could, and stood around the fire, spitting and staring at us. We disliked them intensely.

The building had been part of the Japanese-built Pyongyang medical center. It was a long, massive, four-floored edifice, slightly damaged by one rocket, but on the whole usable and used. Running parallel to this building and connected with it stood another, not forty yards away, equally massive, almost equally intact. The two buildings were surrounded by a large compound and a border of trees which must have made them even more conspicuous from the air. Every time our planes flew over in the daytime we were afraid they might swoop down and blast these buildings. They never did. During heavy night raids, we lay awake, wincing at the rumbling of explosions, thinking—as always happens—that those screaming bombs were coming straight at us. The guards were unconcerned. These buildings, they said, were heavily protected by anti-aircraft guns and U.N. planes did not dare approach.

We wondered, from the first, why we alone had been brought down, and why the others had been left behind. But had the others been left behind? Perhaps they took us to Pyongyang so that we would not witness the departure of the diplomats for home, through China. Why should the authorities take us to Pyongyang before liberating the others, if they were to liberate the others? Why had we thought of such an absurd possibility? Why not stop thinking and wait? Why not stop torturing oneself with baseless speculations? It was very hard to attain such self-discipline, and stop asking questions. All I could do was pretend I had not thought of them, but pretense did not always work.

We plagued our guards with questions. They answered enigmatically. Did they do so because they did not know, reluctant, like all Far Easterners, to lose face by admitting ignorance? Could we take into account the optimistic statement of the Russian-speaking captain? He did not appear particularly bright. Was he just being unjustifiably optimistic, surprisingly kind? Was he trying to make himself interesting? Was there any reason for bringing us down, or was it one of those maddeningly unexplainable moves which in the past had made us suspect the Koreans of acting simply on an impulse which they never follow through.

The second day, January 1, 1952, we were visited by a short, fat, Russian colonel who was trying so hard to be pleasant that we nicknamed him Jovial.

Were we comfortable? Would we like a bath? Would we not do him the favor of shaving our beards? We would look so much more beautiful without beards. Did we have towels and soap? Did we have enough cigarettes?

Yes, yes! But why had we been brought down?

It was not possible to say why. No doubt the highest authority who had taken the decision had good reasons. No doubt the highest authority would tell us when it was time to do so. Meanwhile he, the colonel, was not authorized to tell us. All he could say was that important developments would take place and that we as international journalists were people of international political and propaganda importance who would be released first as soon as the cease-fire agreement was signed.

Why not the diplomats also?

Oh, the diplomats. They too would be released after the cease-fire, but we were more important and, although the colonel was not authorized to say so, we would presumably be released first. Meanwhile the highest authority had given orders that we should be treated very well.

Taking refuge again in safe pessimism, we told ourselves that when we eventually returned to Manpo we would be

able to rag our diplomat friends and tell them they had
been attached to the journalistic group, and not, as they
claimed, the journalists to the diplomatic group.

We were taken out for a walk in the snowy compound
as soon as the fat Russian had gone. We discovered that he
drove up to the Ministry of the Interior every morning in
a United States Army Chevrolet, vanished into the Minister's office, and departed, usually, after an hour's stay.
We knew all about it, of course, and our guards were conscious of our knowledge; nevertheless, great pretense of
secrecy had to be made each morning to keep us from seeing the obese, opulently dressed man whom everyone
treated with such reverence.

We discussed the absurdity of this procedure with a
young, baby-faced lieutenant who seemed to like our
company and kept coming for long exhibitionist discussions, during which he occasionally read the Korean newspapers to us. He said they all realized we knew about the
fat Russian, but it was not "proper" that we should see him
openly, so we were kept in while he was in the neighborhood. This young lieutenant, whom we nicknamed Poupon
because of his extremely juvenile appearance, explained to
us why police officers wore such a queer assortment of
clothes—Army trousers, Security Forces shoulder straps,
civilian cloth caps.

"You see, our lives are in danger. We must be able to
disguise ourselves. So, alone of all the services, we have
the right to wear a varied uniform. Yet people still seem to

recognize us. Only the other night two of our officers were assassinated. I do not understand it."

Poupon was a member of the "intelligentsia." He had been studying economics in the university before the war.

"We had a very good time in the hostels. We ate pure white rice and beef every meal, and we were issued our university uniforms free."

Besides studying, he had been active in various youth movements, and had devoted his spare time to Party work, for which he was rewarded by co-option into the Communist Party of North Korea. He was not sure he would resume his university studies after the war. The work in the security forces was so much more important. And their immediate chief—he belonged to the Intelligence, Counter-Intelligence, and Punitive Branch of the Security Forces—was very remarkable, said Poupon. The chief was not forty yet and he was already a general. A remarkable man the chief, Poupon thought—educated in Germany, trained by the M.V.D. in Khabarovsk for anti-Japanese sabotage, a successful Russian agent, and now one of the most important men in the country.

When we saw Poupon's chief some days later, we recognized in him the unpleasant fat colonel whom we had nicknamed Panjandrum at the dilapidated Pyongyang school where we had been first interned. It was not nice to feel we were directly dependent on the Panjandrum, who was now a prosperous-looking general in a luxurious uniform and an expensive Persian-lamb bonnet. But whatever

we felt about the Panjandrum, his subordinates seemed to
admire him—especially Poupon, who was an enthusiastic
and impetuous young man, strong in his faith, and ready
to believe everything he read in his press. He took as
gospel truth the vituperative North Korean editorials
which accused Syngman Rhee of using Japanese troops to
fight against the country's unity. We pointed out to Poupon that if this were true, the Russian press would surely
have played it up. No Russian paper, at that time, mentioned anything about Japanese in South Korea. This did
not seem to shake Poupon's faith. He could not understand, but he did not doubt.

Poupon's visits to our room were greatly resented by our
two guards, Kim Chin Chun and Han Won Il, who considered us as their personal property—a property which
brought them some prestige and other benefits, in the
form of cigarettes or tobacco, from their curious colleagues
who wanted to view us, and who had to pay for the privilege. This venture of our two guards into show business
made our stay in Pyongyang extremely disagreeable. Not
only did we have the light on constantly for the whole
twenty-four hours to prevent the guard on duty from falling asleep, not only did we have the constant company of
two uninhibited spitters, belchers, and producers of smells,
but we had all their equally uninhibited spitting, belching,
and flatulent friends spending their spare time gaping at
us and asking indiscreet questions about our intimate
habits.

Because our room was warm, it was also used for a study and "political salon"; that is, our guards read aloud to each other the dictation they had taken down during the "politchass"—the political hour. Their courses appeared to deal chiefly with the heresies of the Central and Eastern European Communist parties, and they included such disciplines as memorizing the attacks of Comrade Voulko Chervenko on Kostov. These long Slavonic names tortured the guards, and they appreciated our help in elocution. They tried to learn the English alphabet from us but gave up for fear of losing face when they encountered our labial and dental sounds. At other times they brought us our food and, apparently without resentment, they watched us eat our white rice, meat, and apples, while they had only rough grain and boiled herbs.

Apparently there were orders from the highest authority that we should get good treatment because of our international propaganda importance. Accordingly, the guards tried to do our bidding, but they failed to understand that their constant chanting of Communist texts, their endless comparison of notes on Comrade Chervenko, and the burning light kept us from sleeping or resting. They, who had been brought up with a dozen brothers in the same room, could sleep no matter what. They could sleep with dozens of flies crawling up their nostrils, and they would not wake even when their fellows would roll them over to make some room. Moreover, they did not mind being awakened. Koreans enjoy interrupting their sleep for a chat: it breaks the monotony of the night. They can even go to sleep at will. Their nerves seem to be far less on edge than ours.

It was not possible to convey to them our desire for some privacy. There is no such thing in the Far East, and there is no word for it. The nearest one can get to this English concept is "wanting to be alone so as to do something without being seen"—a suspicious desire on the part of a prisoner.

Exacerbated by their constant presence and lack of Western manners, we retaliated by calling them prison guards. They resented this bitterly, and took endless pains to explain that they were members of the People's Army, that the Security Forces were a part of the Army. When we showed disbelief they sulked silently, thus affording us some minutes of peace. Then, unfortunately, they would remember that the highest authority wanted us to be exceptionally well-treated, so they would come back, amiably offering us their cosmetics, surprised that we would not follow their example and smear evil-smelling pink creams on various parts of our anatomy.

Occasionally, we could get information out of them. They told us that any North Korean serviceman could ask to be demobilized, stating that he no longer wished to serve his country. The request was always granted, they said, and the man was not victimized. He would be handicapped, of course, the guards admitted, because it would become known that he had refused to serve his country, but he had the right to do so. And how about the provision in the constitution which said it was the sacred duty of every citizen to defend his fatherland? They did not know about that, but they did know they could leave the Forces if they wanted to. Did they want to? No, why should they? They were clothed, fed, housed, and given pocket money for much less work than they would have to do as farmers. Moreover, they were important people. They could retire at fifty with pensions and easy jobs as factory watchmen or railway guards. Who would want to leave the Security Forces? What they were worried about was being discharged because of ill-health. They said they were both tubercular. Each time they spat after that, we wondered.

It is said that imitation is a high form of flattery. It is also a form of nuisance, because it brings one's mannerisms sharply to one's notice. The guards watched us and copied us. Han Won Il tried to smoke one of the big pipes we had carved for ourselves. It was an outsize in pipes, by European standards, and its name was "Messalina." Korean pipes take enough tobacco for three puffs only. Feigning sleep, we surreptitiously watched Han Won Il turn pale, then green. He left the room running. We slept a little better that night, but only for a short while, because "Ugly" came.

"Ugly" was the captain of the guard. He was very ugly, very loud, and very puzzled by our reactions to what he considered friendly overtures. That night, noticing finally that we had been wakened by his loud discussion with

208

Kim Chin Chun, he attempted to soothe us by asking us to show him an intimate part of our anatomy. Chagrined by our rude reluctance, he tried to encourage us by giving us the good example. He was told, in vehement but honorific Japanese, by M. Chanteloup, that we were not interested in anatomical comparisons, and he left murmuring that it was impossible to manage these temperamental foreigners.

But if he could not manage us, Ugly could certainly manage the guards, who treated him like a kind of minor deity and seemed to enjoy his squad drill (especially the kind of goose steps practiced by the Red Guards in Moscow) and his demonstrations on how to use the tommygun over rough ground. In particular, he was the idol of the exceedingly juvenile sixteen-year-olds who had arrived with the latest batch of recruits in March 1952. These were children for whom a uniform and a tommygun were marvelous toys. They put on weight on police rations, although these were meager enough.

The new recruits were children, who went birdnesting and played the games of our ten-year-olds. One day Ugly caught them with the eggs they had stolen, and he made them climb back on the trees to replace the eggs. He had heard us telling the young guards birds were useful.

On the morning after he had proposed anatomical comparisons, we asked Ugly for paper. We wanted to write to the Minister of the Interior. Ugly thought ours was going to be a letter of complaints about the episode of the night before, and he refused to give us paper. After a twenty-four-hour hunger strike on our part he gave in, and we wrote to the Minister of the Interior requesting that he forward a document we enclosed to Professor Joliot-Curie of the "World Peace Council" and to the Chairman of the International Red Cross in Geneva. In that document we called upon the two organizations to co-operate for the formation of an agency to handle regular correspondence between captives in Korea and their relatives. We pointed out that either one or the other of the two organizations was recognized by every government in the world, and that consequently they would, by co-operating, produce results. We stated that, in the minds of all the internees and P.O.W.'s, this lack of regular correspondence was an unforgivable cruelty which nullified all attempts at improving the material conditions of captivity. We suggested that to make the work of transport and censorship easier the messages should be written on standard small-size forms, and should be selected from a list of standard messages approved by both sides. We handed this letter to Jovial, the next time we saw him. That was the last we heard of it.

We desperately wanted news from home. This was the spring of 1952, and the negotiations at Kaesong, as reported in the Korean Press, were going through a period of ups and downs. Our guards alternated between gloom and childish optimism:

"The pending questions are nearly settled."

"Everything has gone wrong again."

"Things are once more looking up."

"False alarm, there is no hope."

It was stupid, we knew, to let ourselves be influenced by the reaction of our guards to North Korean propaganda, but we could not help it, because we wanted to be free and we were prisoners. Prison felt more unbearable when Han Won Il was demobilized. He was going home and we felt—felt physically—that we were being left behind. And it was spring again. The few acacias outside the compound were in bloom. Korean urchins were picking the flowers and capering as children will do—lovably, until they saw the "big-nosed foreigners" behind the barbed wire and their shouts of joy turned to screaming insults.

Still, we could not complain, because we were better off than those staggering, skeletic wretches who lived in the part of the building used as a prison. We saw them daily, their hands tied behind their backs, being taken for interrogations, in a room into which we could look. The interrogator screamed, lectured, and slapped. At least we were not subjected to that, nor did we have to carry huge loads, as they did.

One day, one of these prisoners, looking straight at me, while his guard was a few steps away, whistled "Plaisirs d'Amour." Was he trying to convey anything?

If they were not treating us like those other prisoners, we told ourselves, surely they intend to return us some

211

day in the not so distant future. Perhaps the talks will come off after all, and these ups and downs are either horse trading or misinterpretations of the news by the guards. Our next trip to the bath-house, however, filled us with despondency.

Everyone was busy repairing shelters, and government inspectors were supervising the job. Labor was short in North Korea. Why should Ministry of Labor teams of workmen go repairing shelters and dugouts if the Government expected the war to finish soon?

That day we did not sing hymns in our bath, as we had done on other occasions. It was the old woman running the bath who had started us on that habit. She was a Christian. The first time we went there, she sat outside the bathroom and in her high, cracked voice sang: "O God, our help in ages past." We harmonized as best we could. When we went there again she had some of her cronies join in. The guard did not know the songs. He slept in the sun. We were popular at that bath-house. The old woman would scum the water in the round cast-iron tub which had been used by many others before us, and she always wiped the duckboards with a damp cloth. Luckily it was dark in the bathroom and we could not see the water. It smelled pretty bad, but it was hot.

For us, the rebuilding of the shelters was a sure sign. When you do not have the normal type of information, you begin to rely on such signs. We started waiting for the day when we would be sent back to Manpo. Would we be able to go back to that completely uneventful life? Would we not miss all the activity of the capital? After all, there was a lot to see and hear: The confession sessions, when the guards would have to get up, take a bow, applaud themselves, then launch into vehement self-accusation. And the sing-songs that followed, with dance routines by Ugly and Kim Chin Chun. Or the return of the drunkards. Poupon had gone on a spree one night and lost his Party card the next day for "revelry while the country was suffering."

CHAPTER 10

Opéra Bouffe

ONE day Ugly came to tell us that Buchenwald, who had come down for the funds, was to take us back to Manpo. We would be leaving in three days' time, on July 10.

Pyongyang is not very far from the sea. Wading, swimming, or floating down to the Chinan Po gulf on the Tedong River would be a far easier way to escape than any other. Should one attempt the escape? Buchenwald had said the talks had broken down, and that it did not look as if there would ever be peace. Supposing this had become something like Indo-China, was it not one's duty to one's self and to one's family to attempt this escape? Better sleep on it. There are three days to go. Make the decision tomorrow.

That night I had a dream. I was back in naval uniform, and escaping in North Korea, following the banks of the Tedong Gang. Just as I passed a small bend outside Pyongyang, I saw a harbor full of the ships I had known in the Second World War. Their crews were sitting at an

214

open air Hollywood-style cabaret on a low hill by the harbor. There were many whom I knew to have been killed in the war. Someone hailed me, and the tall figure of King Paul of Greece came towards me, in the uniform of an Admiral of the Fleet.

"Where are you going?" he asked.

"I am escaping, sire."

"You shouldn't do that. It is too dangerous."

"But I can't stay in prison all my life."

"You won't. There's no need to try escaping. You will be out by the tenth of April."

"What year?" I asked suspiciously.

"Nineteen fifty-three, of course," said King Paul, and I woke up.

I had taken a purgative for worms the previous day and I felt very weak. The security arrangements of the Koreans appeared very adequate. I was afraid to attempt an escape. Perhaps the dream also influenced my decision not to try, and on the night of July 10, 1952, escorted by Buchenwald, Chanteloup and I started on our way back to Manpo.

The first night we drove for an hour only and stopped at a food depot, not ten miles from Pyongyang, where we slept until we were wakened by the screaming noise of diving jets. We ran for cover and spent the day watching hundreds of bombers with their escorting fighters swooping down on Pyongyang. The ground shook with the sticks of high explosives, and the Chinese soldiers who manned

215

the food depot came up to us and politely expressed their disapproval of the bombing.

Buchenwald told them to leave us alone. All through the trip he squabbled with the Chinese whose interference he resented. He was particularly angered by the insistence of their patrols on checking his identity. He was a sergeant of the police. He was the one to check identities. He was not going to show any papers to any Chinese. Was this Korea or was it China?

His antipathy for the Chinese protected us from a lot of unpleasant curiosity, for the roads and railways were maintained by Chinese troops, who were all curious.

The Chinese system of traffic control was excellent and ensured almost uninterrupted movement day and night. Every third of a mile they had a control post which listened for the sound of planes. As soon as one was heard, the man at the post would fire off his rifle, and this signal would be repeated by all posts that could hear the aircraft. At night, when the rifle shot sounded, all trucks switched off their lights and stopped. In the daytime the trucks took refuge in the numerous drive-in shelters beside the roads. The all-clear was given by whistles, which could be heard when the trucks' engines were not running.

The traffic was heavy, and at every river crossing there was a bridge in operation. We took a long time reaching our destination, because we kept having punctures—once every three hours on an average. The driver, a jolly fellow

216

originating from Seoul, cursed Russian-made tires and re-
gretted bitterly that he was not running an American
truck.

"Russian truck no good," he said, spitting contemptuously on the wheel he was repairing. He had nothing with
which to stick on patches, and was obliged to employ a
vulcanizing technique that consisted of heating a metal
part of the truck with a wood fire, then pressing the
damaged inner tube, with an old piece of rubber as patch,
against the hot metal. The jack was used to provide the
necessary pressure. It looked crude, but it seemed to work.
The patches held. Punctures always appeared in new
places.

The innkeeper at Kaichun, a woman of forty, called me
grandfather, and I did not have a beard then. She meant
to be polite, I'm sure, but nevertheless the comment hurt,
for I was not thirty and I was shocked by my reflection in
the mirror.

A professor from Kangai University was staying at the
inn. He gave us some information on the cease-fire talks,
and spoke proudly of the rising living standards in war-
ravaged North Korea.

"The longer we fight, the longer we can fight. We have
underground factories now which are producing more and
more. You bombed our generators on the Yalu but already
we have restored industrial current and soon we shall
again have electricity for domestic use, as we had two
months ago. We are rebuilding, in spite of your bombing

217

—underground. And we are preparing for the future. Our universities are working dispersed in the villages. We shall not surrender to the dictates of force. We will hold on if necessary until the crisis of capitalism, as predicted by Marx, brings America to her knees."

This sounded an extremely long-term policy to me, and extremely depressing.

"Cheer up," said Chanteloup, himself an ex-professor. "You know what these professors are like when you get onto politics. They are bound to be wrong."

We arrived back at the camp one day too late for what we were told had been Perruche's best Fourteenth of July party to date. Then we were assailed with questions. Among other information, I told the diplomats of my dream about liberation. When the derisive abuse had subsided, Chanteloup and I elaborately explained how Jovial had said we were more important than the diplomats. They staunchly refused to believe there was a man who would hold such an absurd opinion. After that we were given a précis of what had happened in the camp during our absence.

On January 1, 1952, a general had come to the house with an interpreter who spoke violent Brooklynese. A terrific meal was served, then another. The general drank too much.

"Never mind the general," said the interpreter. "He's dead drunk."

The next day the general wanted letters of thanks to Kim Il Sung for the good treatment meted out to the diplomats.

"Good treatment!" Captain Holt had said, in frigid ambassadorial tones. "I suppose you want me to thank His Excellency for the death of Sister Mary Clare, Father Hunt, Father Canavan—not to speak of my colleague the Apostolic Delegate, Bishop Patrick Burns, whom you allowed to die of privations and disease. Good treatment, when you keep me and my colleagues imprisoned against diplomatic practice under the insultingly flimsy pretext that you cannot repatriate us? Shall I include these details in the letter of thanks to His Excellency?"

"Please," said the interpreter, "don't talk like that. You are hurting my feelings."

The general departed without his letters of thanks.

Fatso and the Ripper had had a quarrel, and the latter had stopped being invited for meals, so the rice ration did not fluctuate as much as before. The guards had eaten Bouleau and Dicky, our dogs. In March, thanks to the help of Kuzma, who was still swapping dirty stories with the internees there, the ban on walks had been lifted, and the diplomats had left the courtyard of our house for the first time in over a year. And that was all. The diary kept on the wall by Owen had fifteen entries for six months; eight of these read, "Barber came"; four read, "Cigarettes issued." They had had a quiet life.

It was summer, and during walks up and down our

219

hundred-yard promenade with Captain Holt one could forget captivity as the diplomat went from anecdote to anecdote, from story to story, about the Arab world he knows so well. Then there were Perruche and Meadmore to question on China, and the others. I consider myself lucky to have been interned with people whose varied and extensive knowledge enabled them to help their companions keep mentally alive. Otherwise there would have been nothing but the endless patching and mending of rags.

Electricity came back in October, and went on working. Our planes appeared rarely. Once there was a dogfight and our boys ran. We felt immensely depressed. We were not even cheered up by Ernest's wedding.

It was a magnificent affair. Part of our rations had been systematically stolen for months in advance. The bride was to be one of the sixteen-year-old nurses who ministered to our needs. Ernest's mother lived in the village, and we pitied the poor little girl who was about to become the formidable old woman's slavey.

Ernest had ambitions. He invited many officers. He invited someone who had an accordion. The accordion did not work, but it looked good. Then there was a photographer, and little bridesmaids with baskets made of newspaper, containing confetti. The bride, according to the Korean custom, was carried by the village boys in a closed sedan chair to the schoolhouse where the ceremony was to

take place. The boys were drunk, and the girl hidden in
the sedan must have felt sick. After her came the women
of the village, with their children. Then the men—drunk
as was their privilege—gathered around Ernest, who wore
the village ceremonial suit. This garment, a fiber herring-
bone double-breasted Eastern European creation with im-
posing shoulder scaffolding and bell-bottom trousers, was
worn by the leading personages in all the village dramas.
Bridegrooms, chief mourners—they all wore it. Ernest had
embellished it with a huge rosette of the kind worn by
bulls at agricultural shows. He was as drunk as his guests,
but carried himself with dignity.

At the end of the ceremony the whole village and the
inebriate guests escorted the couple to the home of the
dowager Mrs. Ernest. An hour later, Ernest, looking agitated, came to spend the night in the guardroom. The
gleefully derisive comments and gestures of the French
were obviously understood by Ernest, and went straight
to his heart. The next day the bride, no longer dressed in
her passably smart uniform but in rags, passed our house
repeatedly, carrying enormous loads of firewood, water,
grain. She was being broken in by the dowager Mrs. Ernest who followed, carrying nothing.

Nothing happened then for two months, until the Ripper's grandfather died. As the Ripper's family ruled the
village this was an important event. A man whom we
knew to hold a high position in the local party organiza-

tion was invited down from Manpo. This man supplemented his income as expert in dialectical materialism by being the expert in Taoist sorcery. This was a profitable trade, because he was consulted before each house was built and before each grave was dug. Houses and graves must be oriented in a certain way, to deceive the evil spirits and keep them out. Seeking occasional inspiration in the bottle of rice liquor held by the Ripper, the dialectical-materialist-sorcerer pondered long over the problems of siting the grave. After he indicated the appropriate spot he repaired to the Ripper's house, where he got thoroughly drunk waiting for the hole to be dug. It was already freezing hard, and fires had to be lit over the ground constantly so that the workmen could dig their picks in. When all was ready, the procession started.

The dialectical-materialist-sorcerer headed it, tracing a complicated zig-zag course over the fields so that the evil spirits would have difficulty in following the tracks of the procession. Every now and then he would scatter some imitation coins made of gilt paper. The avaricious evil spirits would stop to pick up the coins and thus lose the scent.

The body was carried shoulder high in a coffin placed inside a rough temple-like structure. There were ropes attached to this "temple" and a group of men pretended they were towing the coffin. Their motions indicated a strong reluctance on the part of the dead man to be removed from his home. Behind the coffin came the wailers, led by the official of the Ministry of Agriculture who normally went about measuring fields and estimating crops for taxation purposes. It was highly formalized wailing that conformed to a recurring pattern of chanting.

After the body was buried, the sorcerer supervised the preparation of a sham grave towards which the evil spirits were directed with arrow-shaped indicator posts. Having thus protected the dead man from dialectical-materialist-Taoist evil spirits, the whole village and the sorcerer got very drunk in the Ripper's house.

Life after that would again have become humdrum, had it not been for Yong Sukee. She was the three-year-old daughter of our cook. Her father had been conscripted by the Communists in Seoul, and the mother had gone north in search of her husband, whose whereabouts she did not discover. Somehow or other this South Korean woman came to be engaged by the guards as cook and general slavey. She needed the job, because her allowance as a soldier's wife was 300 won a month—the price of three apples. At our place she had white rice, firewood, and a billet assigned to her half a mile away. She started work at dawn and went on till late at night, looking after us and the guards.

The cook had no one with whom to leave her child, and little Yong Sukee had to spend the day at our house. The guards would not let the cook sit in the guardroom. Servants had to be kept in their place. The cook and her daughter had their meals in a drafty freezing outhouse. As the weather grew colder, the child became more and more unhappy. She was underdressed and freezing. She cried, and the guards would not have anything to do with her. We made her clothes, and took her in. Owen, an expert father, was in charge during emergencies, when soothing or restraining was needed. The little Korean girl listened wide-eyed to the caressing voice of the big man who held her in his arms, and did what she was supposed to do. At other times she played with the rest of us, especially with Blake, who was the most patient and whom she regarded as her father. She learned a few words of English, gave us nicknames, and dominated much of our existence.

The nights grew much longer, and the interval between the evening meal—which was served at sunset—and breakfast became sixteen hours. The light was too bad for reading, and we knew one another's stories by heart. We had sixteen hours in which to fight against invading thoughts of home. That's why we welcomed the lengthening of the days and the first signs of spring—our third in captivity. No one ventured to make any predictions. The occasional scrap of news we got from Communist sources presented the Korean war as one with no possible issue.

It was hard to keep on hoping.

On March 20, 1953, Captain Holt, Blake, Owen, and I were taken away from the camp. While old Madame Martel was crying, saying good-by, Perruche, trying hard to keep control of his emotions, managed to produce a story which we had not heard before—to send us off with a smile.

We traveled on a special truck. A lieutenant-colonel cadged a ride, in spite of the protests of our escort, who said the truck was especially reserved for us. The lieutenant-colonel promised to keep other hitch-hikers from following his example. A few miles further, a private climbed onto the truck. The lieutenant-colonel ordered him to get down. The private riposted that being a fighting man he had as much right as anyone else to use available transport. The lieutenant-colonel explained the special circumstances. The private said he had to rejoin his unit. The lieutenant-colonel, who was drunk, got angry and screamed at the private. The private screamed at the lieutenant-colonel. A moment later, much to our surprise, they were embracing each other.

"The colonel is drunk," said our escort. "Otherwise he wouldn't shout at the private like that with no reason. Our officers take care of the troops."

"But didn't the private disobey the colonel?"

"No, because he does not belong to the colonel's unit, and the colonel is not in charge of transport anyhow. He can give orders to his men, but only when the business of the unit is involved. And the men of his unit can criticize his orders during the self-criticism hour; but he has no authority over soldiers whom he is not appointed to command."

I had watched North Korean troops comporting themselves creditably under fire in July 1950. If what our escort had said was true, then some Western ideas on military discipline should perhaps be reconsidered.

We arrived in Pyongyang at three in the morning of March 22, 1953. We drove to the Ministry of the Interior, where Chanteloup and I had been interned the year before. The building was still untouched, but we were not allowed in. We drove around the eerie, ruined city, ending up in the well-appointed office of a young captain, who apologized for having no meal ready, handed out cigarettes and offered his bed to Captain Holt. He gave us a November 1951 copy of *U. S. News and World Report.* Tired though we were, we stayed awake till morning, reading the news magazine which had come from the world we had left so many months before. The magazine told us that the Yalu bridges had not been bombed since March 1951, because of Red China's MIG fighters. Could that be true? We found it hard to believe.

The nice young captain said germ bombs had been dropped that night. No, we were not going to be inoculated. Sanitary teams were busy collecting the germs. Then we were taken to a dugout bored into the side of a hill. There a brigadier who looked and acted like Edward G. Robinson in *Little Caesar* personally served us a breakfast of caviar, butter, ham, eggs, spaghetti, cocoa, and petit-beurre biscuits. As the brigadier ran around the table handing us our food, we remembered the days when a mere sergeant had beaten us with the butt of a rifle.

226

Another brigadier appeared on the scene, with three full colonels and a pile of brand-new cotton quilt clothes. One very fat colonel escorted us to a bathroom and himself carried in buckets of water to get the temperature just right. A doctor and a nurse were attached to our staff. A captain and a sub-lieutenant were in constant attendance to provide us with anything we might require.

Did we want anything?

"Please could we have some water to wash our shirts?"

"We would be honored to have your honorable shirts laundered."

"We'd prefer to launder them ourselves. We have only one each, you see, and we can't wait for laundries."

"Only one shirt!" screamed the brigadier. "Bring more shirts for the honorable gentlemen!"

Was there anything else we wanted?

We had forgotten what it is that one wants.

Our resident barber shaved us when we liked. A tailor measured us for suits and overcoats. Magazines, books, newspapers were provided. A movie operator complete with a 35-mm. sound projector and stacks of film joined our retinue. We saw insipid Soviet films, entertaining and colorful shorts of Russian dancing (some sequences with the incomparable Ulanova), Korean newsreels depicting public meetings at which agitators tried to whip up the war-weary civilians to frenzies of hate, and a curiously moving, superbly acted North Korean film of partisan warfare. It had obviously been shot with only one camera, but

227

the principal actors, the supporting cast, and the scenery were real. That film dwarfed the technically superior but completely artificial Soviet productions of *Glinka, Knight of the Golden Star, Happy Market* and Part I of *The Fall of Berlin.*

This fantastic red-carpeting had been going on a week when we were joined by Bishop Cooper, Commissioner Lord, and Monsignor Quinlan, who had arrived in Pyongyang on March 22 and had been kept for six days separated from us in another dugout. We had not seen them for many months and they had a story to tell.

In the summer of 1952 they had been moved from Manpo, where they came under the administration of the Chinese who had been looking after the P.O.W.'s since the autumn of 1951. The standards of living, under the Chinese, rose sharply. More clothes were issued; blankets, quilts, mattresses, towels, soap, toothpaste and brushes, notebooks, pencils, shaving equipment, adequate footwear. Meat became a regular item on the menu; fish, sugar, sweets for the children, cognac for the grown-ups, bread. To us who had lived in the care of Fatso as the "turnip-eating special group of diplomats and journalists," the treatment of the missionaries sounded as incredible as the red-carpeting we were receiving in Pyongyang.

Under the Chinese, the missionaries had been allowed to go for six-mile walks, to sell the supplies they did not need, and to behave pretty much as they pleased. Occasionally they caught glimpses of American and British

P.O.W.'s passing in trucks, looking well dressed and healthy.

For Christmas 1952 and New Year's Day 1953, they were issued much more meat than they could eat. There were over twenty pigs, pheasants, chickens, and geese for the thirty-eight people in the camp. There was more drink, sweets, peanuts.

"No," said the three missionaries in Pyongyang, "after what we've been accustomed to with the Chinese, this red-carpeting, as you call it, does not really impress us."

What could this red-carpeting mean, we asked one another? Not one of us dared give the obvious answer, because we were still afraid of disappointment. Was it to be liberation? Was it possible that the talks were to reach a successful conclusion at last, after all these months of trying? But then, why only the British? Why not bring the French down to Pyongyang as well?

One of the colonels in the dugout kept making long speeches to us, stressing the difference between the British and the Americans. "The British are so much more cultured, so much more mature, so much better behaved, so much more suited by their experience for a leading role than the Americans are. Isn't it unfortunate that the Laborites turned Britain into a satellite of the United States? Imagine all those American troops in Britain playing around with your women! And the burden imposed upon you by the upkeep of Yankee air bases and NATO commitments! It is not possible to believe that a nation with a

229

splendid history like Britain will consent to remain in the humiliating role of a satellite. Soon, she is sure to break away from the Yanks."

Listening to Captain Holt and Bishop Cooper defending the American people they had met, we tried to read between the lines of the colonel's speech.

Was the good colonel merely repeating Stalin's latest pronouncements on the inherent differences of the capitalist world and trying to help a little, with his speeches to us, in worrying out the policy of the "Father of the People"? Or was it possible that an Anglo-American break was about to take place? What our French colleagues would say about *"La perfide Albion,"* in such an event, we did not care to think.

Then the nurse let a list fall from her pocket. On it we saw, after ours, the names of the French. We noticed that food trays containing rations similar to ours, and in numbers corresponding to the numbers of French colleagues, were being taken somewhere three times a day from our kitchens. So, whatever the game was, it included the French. Were both Britain and France going to break with the United States?

The "Anglophile" colonel asked us to write an appreciation of the treatment we had received in North Korea. He did not respond to our hints that such statements should be written only immediately before liberation. Following Captain Holt's lead, we gave a brief factual description of the treatment we had received. Captain Holt wrote about the death march, and about the loss of his nationals. The colonel did not appear to like our papers, but he did not ask us to write new ones.

He submitted me to two cross-examinations, the main purpose apparently being to elucidate whether at the front in Korea I had been a civilian or a member of the U. S. Armed Forces. Had I been properly accredited? Had I had honorary rank? Had I had U. S. identification documents? I maintained, as I had done at every inter-rogation, that I had been an unarmed civilian, uncon-nected with the United States Army, possessing only the credentials issued by my paper, and arrested, to my mind, illegally, by the North Korean forces while I was not within their frontiers.

"Other correspondents captured at the front," said the colonel in a voice which sounded ominous to me, "have been put in P.O.W. camps."

That is what I had always feared from the beginning, believing that as a civilian I stood a better chance of early release. Deep inside, I believed that the red-carpeting was a prelude to liberation. Were the authorities going to change their mind at the last minute and send me to re-join my unfortunate colleagues in the P.O.W. camps, in-stead of releasing me with the civilians? I worried, unnec-essarily, until the day we crossed the frontier.

At the evening meal of April 7, the English-speaking

major who acted as our interpreter told us that the mor-row would be the most beautiful day in our lives. Later, representatives of the Korean Press came to interview us. They were headed by the correspondent of the *Labour Journal*, the *Pravda* of North Korea.

"We have come," said this gentleman, "to talk with you in an atmosphere of freedom and to ask you a few ques-tions." He poured out beer and handed round a plate of biscuits. "First," he continued, "I want to ask Captain Holt what he thinks about the way he has been treated in North Korea."

"As a member of Her Majesty's Foreign Service, I am not allowed to express opinions without previous consulta-tion with my Government, and certainly not to the press."

"Could you tell us what your opinion is of the barbarous, murderous American bombing?"

"I have already answered all your questions. I cannot say more."

"We think you can say more."

"I am grateful to you for disclosing your thoughts to me."

The North Korean journalists shifted their attack. "You, Mr. Deane," they said, "are a journalist. At the truce talks we have always been able to discuss freely with our col-leagues of the capitalist press. We are sure that we can talk with you in the same way. What do you think of the treatment you received?"

"No comment."

232

"What do you think of the criminal American bombing?"

"No comment."

"Why will you not answer our questions?"

"No comment."

They tried to put words into the mouths of the missionaries in condemnation of the Americans, and received no answer. When the missionaries started replying "no comment," the senior journalist turned to me:

"Have you taught them that?"

"No comment."

Then they tried to get statements out of Blake and Owen, who replied that if there was anything to say Captain Holt would say it.

"Are you afraid to talk in front of Captain Holt?"

"No comment."

"We," said the representative of the *Labour Journal*, "came here to speak in an atmosphere of freedom. The British journalists we have met at the truce talks always boast that there is freedom in Britain. But we find no freedom here."

"That is quite correct," said Captain Holt. "Seven of us are not free men."

The next morning, the brigadier told us that following a request from the British Government, transmitted to Pyongyang by the Russian Government, the Korean People's Democratic Republic had decided to release us. That night we would leave for the Chinese border.

This day which was to have been the most beautiful of our lives was one of anticlimax, for we still did not believe.

Attended by our numerous retinue, we changed, put on new underclothes and suits. Our fingers went through the forgotten motions of shaping the knots of our ties.

"Ah," said the doctor, looking at us, starry-eyed, "you gentlemen now."

Outside, nothing daunted by their defeat of the night before, our friends of the Korean press were waiting, flanked this time by a platoon of cameramen. They tried hard again to provoke us into statements condemning the Americans, and were met by a barrage of "no comment." Finally, Captain Holt grew tired of it.

"Look here," he said, "you go on chattering about peace, democracy, and international understanding. What are you doing to achieve any of these objectives? You could do much by supplying accurate information on which understanding can be based. Instead, you just fill your columns with abuse, and try to elicit from us some statement you could enlarge into anti-American propaganda. If you want peace and international understanding, why do you not concentrate on information rather than abuse? Why don't you give us some information so we can pass it on and help our people understand yours? Why not tell me, for instance, the details of your agrarian reform, or the main features of your constitution? What is your social security like?"

"Please," said the journalists, "we have come to interview you, not to answer questions. Besides, we are not authorized to tell you such things."

"Aha," said Captain Holt, "and how about this atmosphere of freedom you talked about so eloquently last night?"

The journalists departed.

"They didn't even have the sense," said Captain Holt, "to separate us so that we would not have witnesses to deny the lies they will attribute to us."

That night we drove to the frontier. We had come down the Manpo-Pyongyang road to the northern capital, and we went to the Chinese frontier along the Pyongyang-Antung road. All the bridges on both roads were functioning. We passed many trains. Trucks followed one another in procession. Between Pyongyang and the frontier, on the night of April 8, I counted more than 1,000 trucks going south.

"The communications," a Korean colonel told me, "are working as they have never worked before."

And along the road, on both sides, every town, every village was completely destroyed. Somehow it did not make sense.

The North Korean customs went through us with a fine-toothed comb. Sewn into pads shaped like my calves, I carried on me, strapped below the knees, a large quantity of writing which I wanted to keep. In a bag, I had a much larger amount of writing—odd exercises, notes on Marx,

235

and the like. These I did not want to keep. Assisted by Commissioner Lord (who was interpreting) and according to a prearranged plan, I protested vehemently against surrendering the notes I had in my bag. The Koreans were very insistent, and so was I. I even hinted that I would refuse to go home if my notes were confiscated. The brigadier who was escorting us, and who was in a "red-carpeting" frame of mind, cursed the wretched customs official who was doing his job. Finally a compromise was reached. They would read the notes, they said, and send them on. Could I please give them an address? Yes, I wanted a receipt. The ruse had worked. Unnerved by the hysterical argument, the customs official did not search me. Determinedly clutching the bag with my unwanted notes, he watched me crossing the frontier. I like to think that some poor Korean interpreter is wading through page after page of bad handwriting between the lines of *Das Kapital,* trying to discover the hidden meaning behind remembered quotations of Anacreon's erotic poetry, obtuse clues for crosswords, attempted translations of the Gospel from the United States Army version back into Alexandrine Greek, criticism of Communist classics and some of Perruche's juiciest stories.

CHAPTER 11

Siberia, Moscow, Home

WE CROSSED the Korean-Manchurian frontier on April 9.

"King Paul of Greece," said Blake, reminding me of my dream, "was right. You've been freed before the 10th."

And so the Koreans themselves finally shattered their version of why we had been kept prisoners so long: "Kept under the protection of the North Korean Government, until the barbarous American bombing should stop, with the cease-fire, so that the internees could travel safely to the frontier" (Pyongyang *Labour Journal,* January 26, 1952).

Here we were at the frontier, safe, and there had been no cease-fire.

Why had we been kept? The Communists had admitted that we had no exchange value as hostages. Had we been interned and almost killed for the reason hinted at by Mr. Vishinsky in Lake Success? Had we been buried alive for nearly three years as a revenge for the internment by the British, in 1920, of the Soviet Mission to Teheran?

The Chinese control made not the slightest difficulty.

A young English-speaking Chinese met us, welcomed us, and in luxurious American-made cars whisked us off to the best hotel in town. There we were greeted by Mr. Pyotr Fyodorovich Vassilief, who introduced himself as a member of the Russian Embassy in Peking. Debonair, friendly, yet restrained, he made us feel we could call on him and that we needn't fear any intrusion on his part. We had a wonderful time in a huge communal bath, brimful with hot water. Scented soap and freshly laundered towels were provided, and we just let ourselves soak. In another part of the building a Chinese concert party was singing. Suddenly all of us rediscovered one of the basic urges which grip the Western male. We had to sing in our bath. Led by Bishop Cooper, we went into verse after verse of "Who Killed Cock Robin?" and "Three Blind Mice," finishing up with a deafening rendition of "Land of Hope and Glory." The Chinese concert party was silenced.

When we left the bathroom members of the concert party had gathered outside to see us. We kept our eyes lowered.

That evening, in our luxurious limousines, we were driven to the well-kept Japanese-built railway station of Antung. We were expected. A procession of officials escorted us to a special car. It had a club car with deep, soft armchairs—you must sit on the floor for nearly three years to be able really to appreciate an armchair. There were chicken and caviar and all sorts of drinks on the table. There were silent-footed, obsequious waiters, and there

238

were inviting berths in tastefully decorated compartments. Pyotr Fyodorovich Vassilief talked books, music, ballet, sport, without once introducing the too familiar Soviet slant into his conversation. He was soothing—we were grateful. After a night in our frothy berths we arrived at Mukden, where we were whisked away again by enormous sedans to a well-appointed hotel. Rooms with private bathrooms, a paneled private dining-room, and any kind of food we could think of. Unfortunately, we did not yet know what we wanted, and we kept embarrassing our hosts by enquiring whether it was permissible for us to have a bath, and whether we could really go into the neon-and-nickel barber shop for a shave.

Since we were staying thirty-six hours, we asked to see the town, and it was tactfully explained to us that ours would be a "conducted tour." We were driven in lovely vehicles, slowly, through the best districts of the Japanese-built part of Mukden. The old Chinese walls were being demolished. We were not shown antiquities. My guide said the New China was more interesting than the Old China. At all street intersections the small pavilions for the traffic policemen were decorated with plaster Picasso doves, and attractive Chinese characters writing "peace" in every imaginable way.

We passed many shops. Their windows were full of production posters, of advertisements. There were very few actual goods.

On the clean, well-kept sidewalks, Monsignor Quinlan,

an old China hand, saw something which surprised him. "Bedad!" he said. "Look at those girls, their feet unbound, their heads high, their little chests stuck out, walking freely. They look happy now. Not like the poor little things I knew before, trailing behind their popos." ("Popo" is Chinese for mother-in-law.)

Back in the hotel, the representatives of a big department store brought us samples of their wares. They gave us women's knee-length stockings. Most of their goods were of very poor quality. The razors they gave us removed the skin from under one's beard, but not the beard. The zip-bags fell to pieces the first night. The only articles of really good quality were some exquisite but gaudy Chinese brocade dressing gowns. A group of normally inhibited Englishmen slipped into these gorgeous garments, and struck attitudes in front of the full-length mirrors. Then, as if by common consent, they looked at one another. The pleased, exhibitionist smiles were replaced by the normal expressions worn by people in their position. "Ridiculous!" they said. "Couldn't possibly wear such a ghastly thing."

We were then taken to a beautiful blue train, spoiled only by bad reproductions of that shaggy Picasso dove. This was the "Peace Express," Red China's show train, which carried us—running dead on time—to the Sino-Soviet frontier town of Manchu Li. There we spent part of the day in a hotel which we shared with an Outer Mongolian concert party, whose male members were busy smearing cold cream on to their faces in the bathroom, and dousing themselves with potent perfume. Finally we crossed into Russia. In the frontier town of Otpor, a strikingly handsome Intourist official told us the surprising—and a little alarming—news that henceforth we would not be escorted. He gave us a credit account for the restaurant car, and a thousand rubles to spend on incidentals. The customs processed us, an exceedingly courteous and well-dressed official looked at our papers, and a young doctor with a pleasant bedside manner took our temperatures and inquired solicitously after our health. Then the train started.

That night while I stood in the corridor a six-year old boy came and started talking to me. He did not have straight, black hair and slanted eyes. He was fair and blue-eyed. He did not scream "big-nosed foreigner" at me. This little boy called Boris made me feel near to freedom at last.

The train had two types of carriage, marked "Hard" and "Soft." In the "hard" carriages the passengers had to provide their own bedding for the wooden berths; in the "soft," sheets and blankets were available to cover the innerspring beds. In our "soft" carriage there was a sergeant of the Red Army. In the "hard" carriage ahead there was a major of the Red Army Tank Corps. In our "soft" carriage, along with doctors, engineers and other University-standard technicians returning from advisory duties in China, there were locomotive firemen. In the "hard" carriages, along with locomotive firemen, there were intellectuals.

The end carriage was an old pre-Revolution *wagon-lit* car, reserved for three men who, alone in the train, wore made-to-measure suits. The other passengers were not allowed to go into that car. Yet these three—whom we, of course, called "the commissars"—came to eat with everyone else in the dining car. As soon as they were seated, the attendant brought them linen napkins; everyone else used paper. The fourth chair at their table was occupied by whoever came first—by a locomotive fireman, by a Red Army private, by a colonel, once by a dowdy woman who acted like a prostitute.

The dining car was in plastic and chrome. Not everyone used it. Many people bought their food at the stations—boiled potatoes, sauerkraut, yoghurt, bread, smoked herrings, pieces of boiled meat. "The commissars" from the special car sometimes bought boiled potatoes at the stations.

The waiters and waitresses, when they made out their bills, sat down at the table beside their customers and joked with them. Then they would accept a tip with a low bow and rush to open the door. One of the dining-car attendants walked up and down the corridors of the train with a basket, selling oranges. We called her "Nell Gwyn." At every station, Nell Gwyn rushed out on to the platform offering her wares: she said she wanted to exceed her sales norm. The people in the stations bought readily from her, and from the peasant women selling local produce at various stands. They were warmly but untidily clad. They wore top boots or Wellingtons which, by and large, seemed to be of good quality.

Standing under huge slogans proclaiming that Stalin was "immortal," that he would "live for ever," the people at Chita station addressed us with aggressive friendliness. Five gigantic Red Army lieutenants surrounded Bishop Cooper and told him that an old gentleman like him should not smoke. Smoking was bad, they said, but drinking vodka was fine. These same young officers warned me not to try taking any Communist publications into Britain; if I did, I would be arrested on arrival. They listened politely but with incredulous expressions when I told them that the *Daily Worker* was on sale everywhere in Britain, and that at Collet's you could buy all the Communist publications.

"That was three years ago," they said. "You will find things changed."

When I asked them why their bookstalls had no non-Communist publications on sale they replied: "We don't need them. Our press tells us the truth."

From the windows of our compartment we watched train after train pass us, going east. There were great numbers of brand-new trucks, bridge sections, field artillery, tractors, pumping-station equipment, coal, oil, reels of wire, steel slats, packing cases. On the cars, in chalk, were marked the destinations of the freight. The field guns were marked "Korea," the tractors were marked "China."

The quantity of rolling stock was impressive. There seemed to be an abundance of locomotives, some reminiscent of Stephenson's Rocket, others huge, powerful brutes that looked capable of moving mountains.

"These," said an engineer, showing us a group of big locomotives at a siding near Irkutsk, "are American. They came during the war."

"Are they good?"

"Very good."

Every now and then we passed enormous airfields, outside Chita, Irkutsk, Krasnoyarsk, Omsk. There were planes on the fields, but they were too far away to be identified.

All bridges were guarded by armed sentries.

After Novosibirsk, and all the way to Moscow, we passed enormous plowed fields. We saw a number of Machine and Tractor Stations with long lines of mechanized agricultural equipment. We saw long belts of trees planted around those fields, and were told they were wind-breaks.

At Krasnoyarsk, Novosibirsk, Omsk, Sverdlovsk, we rolled past huge factories, metallurgical and chemical plants. From Krasnoyarsk westwards one had the impression that there was a lot of heavy industrial development. In between the towns there was steppe land or forest— chiefly birch trees. Sometimes the train's loudspeakers would play haunting Russian melodies that seemed to blend with the landscape.

A locomotive engineer came into the compartment I

shared with Commissioner Lord, Bishop Cooper and Monsignor Quinlan. The engineer was very drunk, and very friendly. He sat between the bishop and the commissioner and, embracing the latter, kissed him repeatedly all over his head. Then came the Bishop's turn. I climbed on to the top berth, exposing Monsignor Quinlan, who had been sheltering behind my back.

"Philip, my boy," said the Monsignor, trying to extricate himself from the arms of our guest, "how could you desert me like this after what we have been through together?"

Captain Holt came in to ask a question. He was immediately seized by the ears and kissed energetically on the top of the head.

"From Russian literature," said Captain Holt, wiping his head, "one gathered that Siberia was full of gloomy, unrecognized prophets. Instead, we find it full of drunken engineers."

Commissioner Lord tried to sneak out of the compartment. Our merry guest stretched a hairy, brawny hand into the corridor and firmly drew the reluctant commissioner back into his arms. Holding firmly on to the commissioner with one hand and on to the bishop with the other, and punctuating his remarks with sonorous, humid kisses, the engineer delivered a three-hour speech, the gist of which seemed to be a sort of conjugation:

"I am a good man:
You are a good man;

245

> He is a good man;
> We all are good men, etc."

and

> "I love peace;
> You love peace;
> He loves peace;
> We love peace, etc."

Next day he came to apologize. He hoped he had not offended us. He hoped that the commissioner had not minded being kissed. I assured the engineer that Commissioner Lord had enjoyed every embrace. Then we had a long talk.

He was a Ukrainian who had gone to school for seven years, then to a railway-training establishment for three. After two years' apprenticeship he had become a fully-fledged engineer. His salary was 1,200 rubles a month. For fuel economy and running on time, he said, he received a monthly bonus of 600 rubles, handed to him at a ceremony with a band playing, red banners, speeches, and vodka. At the end of the day's run he could wash and change at the railwaymen's hostel, where there was also an inexpensive canteen. His working clothes were provided, as was the watch he proudly wore on his wrist. He had been to Siberia on a special one-month assignment for which he had been paid an extra 1,700 rubles, and was now returning to the Ukraine, where his wife—a railway worker earning 700 rubles a month—waited for him.

He and his wife went to the movies twice a week (the seats cost from two to three and a half rubles). They had a small four-room house.

"Not a wooden one like these," he said, pointing out of the window to the tiny dilapidated shacks lining the un-paved quagmires that seemed to serve as roads in Siberia, "but built with stones, with a garden in which the blos-soms are now coming out. I pay fifty rubles a month rent and in ten years the house is mine. If I wanted, I could borrow 10,000 rubles from the Government and have my own house built the way I want. The carpenters and masons would do as I tell them. I'd have to repay the loan in ten years, with no interest. But, of course, I have a high salary. The average salary is 750 rubles a month."

(The housing we saw in Siberia was of a very low standard. Commissioner Lord of the Salvation Army told me: "My work has been in the slums. I've never seen in Britain a slum that could compare with these.")

Our engineer friend said that he could buy a working suit, ready-made, for 100 rubles, and that he had bought a Sunday-best for 500.

"I look beautiful in it," he said, smiling reminiscently. Then he left us.

The train stopped at various stations for periods of up to thirty minutes. We were amazed to find that we could walk out into the towns, ask questions, look at prices, without any interference from the black-uniformed militia-men. In Tatarskaya I went into a store where shoppers

247

were showing a kind of pass to the saleswoman before buying. Women's sandals, of very poor quality, were from forty-five to sixty-five rubles. Rough calico dresses for three-year-old girls, in "screaming" colors, fifty-five to seventy rubles. Knitted cotton sweaters for women, eighty-five rubles.

At Omsk, in a food store, prices I noted were as follows: One egg, 1 ruble 30 kopeks; one kilogram of sugar, 11 rubles 80 kopeks; one kilogram of veal, 15 rubles; one kilogram of biscuits, 26 rubles 80 kopeks; one kilogram of butter, 28 rubles; one pint of milk, 3 rubles 85 kopeks; one pint of yoghurt, 10 rubles 30 kopeks; cigarettes (red pack called Drug), 4 rubles 50 kopeks; one pint of ordinary white wine, 11 rubles; one pint and a half of champagne, 30 rubles; one ounce of caviar, 7 rubles; one cooked steak, 6 rubles; one plate of borshch soup, 6 rubles.

At Tumen, shoes were sold on the station. People bought them at a stand without showing any pass. This time, the prices for women's sandals of very cheap quality ranged from 450 rubles; men's shoes, of a quality lower than anything I have seen in Britain, from 465 rubles.

I was desperately in need of paper to make notes, but I found some only at Sverdlovsk, where I bought a drawing album. A penholder and pen point cost four rubles.

Other prices I noted on the journey were: half-pound jar of honey, 13 rubles 60 kopeks; margarine, 15 rubles a kilogram; watches of very shoddy quality, 375 rubles for the cheapest; teddy bear of cheap black plush, 45 rubles;

piano accordion in general store at Kirov, 907 rubles; cloth-faced dolls of very poor quality, starting at 56 rubles; basic railway fare from Manchurian frontier to Moscow, 397 rubles, plus 443 rubles extra for "hard" sleeper and 750 rubles extra for "soft" sleeper; luggage on same journey, 15 rubles 41 kopeks extra for each five kilograms.

At the first small station after Chita a girl with no arms was begging. A militiaman, pointing to us, told her to leave the station.

At Udinsk, an old blind beggar, kneeling on the platform, was asking God to bless those who were giving him alms. One of the "commissars" from the *wagon-lit* car gave him some kopeks. The beggar blessed Monsignor Quinlan and Commissioner Lord, each of whom gave him a ruble.

At Krasnoyarsk a blind beggar, a young man wearing a Red Guardsman's badge, came on to the train guided by a boy of about twelve. He went from compartment to compartment getting alms. The car attendant told him to go to another part of the train because there were some "English delegates" in the car.

We asked an engineer, returning home after two and a half years in China, why there were beggars. He said everyone could work, even blind people, but there were some who did not want to work, and it was not possible to coerce them. Yet at Tumen two girls of ten were begging. This our engineer friend did not explain.

Sverdlovsk had a huge station building. It is an important junction. On the square outside the station, long lines of people were waiting with bundles, suitcases, baskets. Some were sleeping on the concrete sidewalk. The station had two floors. On the ground floor there was a waiting room. Commissioner Lord and I were sickened by the smell when we entered. Children in dirty clothes, some barefoot, their legs soiled, were playing among the helpless bodies of the drunks. The smell of cheap spirits, vomit, and dirty diapers that were being dried was overpowering. An old gipsy woman, sitting on the floor, was examining her jacket for insects. We went out. Over the door of the waiting room we had left there was a sign: "Waiting Room, Second Class." Beside it, over another door, was another sign: "Restaurant, First Class." In that restaurant there were tables covered with white linen, expensive silver, wine glasses, and good china. Smartly uniformed waitresses served men and women in rich clothes, jewelery, and too much perfume. Outside a legless man with a medal on his chest was dragging himself along on a sort of leather pad. He was not begging. We went back to the platform. Under a sign marked: "No Quarreling" two of the numberless drunks one saw everywhere were unsuccessfully trying to hit each other. A militiaman looked on tolerantly. The train conductor told us to get on, and we went apprehensively to the restaurant car to resume with the cashier the feud we had started on April 15. He had approached us that day during supper.

"You," he said, in a loud, accusing voice, "are not fulfilling the plan."

There was one of those awful silences. Every diner

250

paused and looked at us. A young mother raised her child above her head and pointed to us. To be accused of not fulfilling the plan is a terrible stigma in Russia. We lowered our eyes before all those accusing glances.

"You," continued the cashier, "are not fulfilling the eating norm set for you by Intourist. You have been prisoners. You must recuperate. You must eat much. You must eat 420 rubles-worth a day, and you are nowhere near that figure. Why?"

"Everything," we answered sheepishly, "is very expensive and as we might have to pay for it we cannot afford these things."

One of the diners intervened.

"You see," he explained to the cashier, gesturing broadly, "they are afraid they might have to reimburse the Soviet Government."

We looked at that man gratefully. It was nice to get some moral support.

"I don't know about that," said the cashier. "Intourist says they must recuperate and they will not eat. Is our cooking not good?" The cook glared at us from the service hatch. "Is the comrade waitress not attending them properly?" The comrade waitress appeared mortally offended. "And," added the cashier, gesturing dramatically and looking around the car for approval, "I put it to you, comrades, are not our Soviet products the best in the world?"

With this last tirade, he swung the audience to his side. A censorious murmur arose from the other tables.

"I," said the cashier, setting his jaw grimly, "will see

that you fulfil your plan." Turning to his staff, he ordered: "Serve."

As we plowed through course after course, as we drank bottle after bottle of champagne, the glares on the faces of our fellow diners disappeared, to be replaced by encouraging smiles. Like spectators at a football game, they egged us on, sending an occasional gift bottle to show their appreciation of our efforts. With perspiration pouring from our foreheads we persevered, feeling that Anglo-Soviet relations were at stake. That night, our two compartments were every bit as noisy as the neighboring ones. If our drunken engineer friend had passed our door, he would have been made to pay.

The next morning, of course, we could not eat, and at lunch we had another lecture. Sitting at our table, we could not grasp the reality of this *opéra-bouffe* train which flashed past the Siberian forests, its loudspeakers playing oompah-pah music and its occupants conjugating Russian verbs at the slightest provocation:

> "I love peace
> You love peace
> He loves peace,
> We love peace."

When I told a lady engineer that Stalin's pamphlet on *Dialectical Materialism* could not really be considered to be philosophical writing, tears came to her eyes and she said: "You must not speak like that about him. It is wicked."

At last we reached Moscow, dazed, overfed, amazed at the freedom with which we had been allowed to investigate everything. And there at the station, too poignantly British for words, a group of truly friendly people, smiling, trying hard and unsuccessfully to control their emotions, just took us over. We felt that this was very near to freedom. The next day, having been feted by the Ambassador as we had never been feted before, we were driven to the airport.

There, amid the Soviet planes, a silver bird with the red, white, and blue roundels which had marked the wings of the "Few," was waiting for us. Coddled by the crew, the doctor and the nurse, airborne at last, we began to understand that the dreams we had seen shattered so often had at last come true.